7.94

HOW TO CLIMB
YOUR FAMILY TREE

Harriet Stryker-Rodda

HOW TO CLIMB YOUR FAMILY TREE

Genealogy for Beginners

G.K.HALL &CO.
Boston, Massachusetts
1990

Published in Large Print by arrangement with
Genealogical Publishing Co.

G.K. Hall Large Print Book Series.

Set in 18 pt Plantin.

Library of Congress Cataloging in Publication Data

Stryker-Rodda, Harriet.
    How to climb your family tree : genealogy for beginners / Harriet
Stryker-Rodda.
        p.   cm.—(G.K. Hall large print book series)
    ISBN 0-8161-5006-0 (lg. print).—ISBN 0-8161-5021-4 (pbk.: lg. print)
    1. Genealogy.   2. United States—Genealogy—Handbooks, manuals,
etc.   I. Title.
[CS16.S858   1990]
929'.1'072073—dc20   90-32772

CONTENTS

Introduction

Genealogy and family history received an impetus from the nation's Bicentennial celebration that has made them of interest to a larger number of people than ever before—in fact, genealogy is now the nation's most popular hobby. The desire to know themselves and their origins, to learn from whom they acquired the genes that make them unique, has made eager searchers of thousands of citizens who are seeking answers to questions about their heredity: how much were their ancestors influenced by their environment—the climate, the culture in which they lived, their social and economic status—and how much were they affected by their inherited genes? These questions and many more have brought interested searchers to the pursuit of their beginnings in other countries as well as in America, to satisfy their curiosity about how they came to be what they are.

If you count the number of people whose

blood flows in your veins, you notice that, in the first generation back, there were only your two parents whose genes contributed to your genetic makeup. In the second generation back, your grandparents' generation, there were four people, and in the third generation back, eight, and so on. The number keeps doubling in geometric progression, so that as recently as six generations ago there were sixty-four people from whom you could trace your descent. Viewed another way, it took, in only six generations (added up: 64 + 32 + 16 + 8 + 4 + 2), 126 people to make you genetically what you are.

And that's what genealogy is all about: learning to know those people. Where did they live? When did they enter and leave their world? What did they do to support themselves and their children? What were they really like? What was their world like? How different was it from the one in which you live? (This is particularly important in our increasingly automated, computerized world.) Why does your mother shake her head and say, "You are just like your Great-uncle John!"? Are there persistent family characteristics that can be traced? Are we subject to hereditary ills or tendencies toward them? Do you love to carve wood because someone in your family before you was a woodcarver? One of the most fascinating puzzles in the world is *your* family. It is not like anyone else's family. To search for even one member, to place him in the period in history when he lived, to dress him in the clothes of his time, to follow his footsteps through his world, is a thrilling and rewarding experience.

It is also great fun. Searching for stories about our ancestors satisfies that curiosity everyone has, even though not everyone will admit to having it. It's fun to talk with relatives you have never known before, to realize that you are kin. It is fascinating to visit the homes of distant cousins and see how similar or different they are from you. Imagine the delight in discovering an old box or two of pictures that show your common ancestors in various stilted poses and costumes. All sorts of interesting and unusual things happen to you, to your self-awareness, when you begin to try out your detecting skills.

Tracing a family's genealogy is a hobby anyone can pursue because we all descend from people who have passed through this world before us. Anyone can reach out to touch *some* of them. If you're lucky and have the time, it's usually even possible to locate and claim *many* of them. The challenge is part of the fascination of the work. Furthermore, it's an activity that calls for no special talents. You don't even need specialized tools. A pencil and notebook are sufficient to start with. If you can write and record accurately in a notebook what you find or are told, you need no other skills to start you.

Another attraction is that there is no boss standing over you to make you work. You are your *own* boss. You set your own pace. How much time you give your research, when you work at it, how quickly you produce results are all up to you. Granted, there is no paycheck for the work you accomplish, but the satisfaction and rewards inherent in the work more than outweigh that drawback. Some people become temporarily frustrated when data prove elusive, but the satisfaction lies in the intelligent search, in locating missing information, in bringing an ancestor back into the family circle where he belongs, and in proving that he and you belong together. That satisfaction is reward in itself. It makes the searcher feel great, proud of being a good sleuth and confident that other problems can be solved.

Genealogy is not something new that has

just sprung full-blown in our modern day. The subject of genealogy is of such innate human interest that it must have begun with the first family. As the family grew, and the children themselves began to look for mates, and the children's children, each new generation must have said, "Tell me about your mother and father. What was it like when you were little?" Even before man had learned to write, genealogy was born. The Old Testament is full of family tracing. Genealogy, in however crude a form, was important to the tribes of Israel.

Today genealogy is recognized as a science. It uses all the techniques that any other science employs: research to discover what has been previously proved; building on that to discover new data; analysis of old and new research to discover weaknesses and strengths; synthesis to pull old and new together and complete the product. At its best it follows scientific methods: it begins with the known and works toward the unknown. Searching for ancestors involves the use of many disciplines; history, geography, mathematics, law, religion, and more all become the tools of the persistent searcher. As a family sleuth you can sometimes uncover those secrets, those pockets of unknown details that allow you to understand the conditions and times in which your forebears lived. Their successes will add to your ancestors' luster; their failures will make them more real. Perhaps you will find their successes and failures reflected in you and in other members of your family. Learning to know yourself in this way will give more pleasure than you think. Great personal insights can result from your research, and you will meet many fine people along the way.

Harriet Stryker-Rodda
Certified Genealogist

HOW TO CLIMB
YOUR FAMILY TREE

PART ONE
Doing Your Own Research

1

Beginning with Yourself

Open your left hand. Let your middle finger represent yourself. Let the index finger represent your parents; the thumb, your grandparents. Let the ring finger represent your children if you have any, and the little finger, your grandchildren. Your right hand can represent your spouse's family in the same way. Looking at the long middle finger, you can see how, as middleman, you are in a position, usually from your own knowledge, to re-create three generations—yours, your parents', and your grandparents'. Add to that the knowledge of your children and grandchildren as they arrive and you and your spouse, the middlemen, will each become the link among five generations. Together the two of you can supply knowledge of six generations —that is, three on your side and three on his or hers—to two current generations: your children and grandchildren. Gathering that

3

knowledge to pass on is the beginning of the search into your family's history.

In terms of equipment, genealogy is a fairly simple hobby. At the start, essentially all you need are a pencil and a notebook. Then, as progress is made and the facts begin to pour in, you will need a real system and a corner in which to store your growing mass of documents and records.

The very first step, then, is to write down what you know about yourself. In some ways this may be the easiest and most rewarding part of your search, for hidden in what may seem like the unimportant facts of your life are clues that can help you uncover the details of generations past. Don't be bashful. Write down everything you can think of. It needn't be elaborate, but on the other hand the more you can remember about the whos, whens, and wheres of your life, the more facts you will have to work with. Just start with what is pertinent and go on from there with whatever embellishments you want to add.

Begin with where and when you were born. What was your father's name? Your mother's? What was her maiden name? Were you baptized, christened, or Bar Mitzvahed? Where? When? Were you married? More than once? Divorced? What is (are) the full name(s) of your spouse(s)? Are you still single? An opening paragraph for your autobiography might read something like this:

Shirley Margaret Peters, third child and second daughter of Charles Spencer and Margaret (Dorman) Peters, was born 10 April 1903 in South Parma, Missouri, baptized 14 June 1917 at the First Baptist Church of South Parma; married 20 July 1924 by Melvin Spicer, Justice of the Peace, in Luden, Illinois, to James Sylvester Helms, born 5 July 1901 in San Jose, California, the oldest son of Bernard Carmichael and Lorena (Sylvester) Helms.

After this kind of opening paragraph, any kind of narrative can be developed, telling about things you remember, anecdotes about another generation, and stories about parents and grandparents, brothers and sisters. Anything you want to share is suitable for inclusion in your autobiography. No one else can write it as you can, because no one else has had your particular experience. This is the place where you can record not only the important events in your life, such as graduation, college, travel, honors, but also

5

the ordinary happenings. Sometimes—especially in this day and age—it's the small things developing slowly over time that have the greatest impact on our lives. One elderly lady took as the theme for her autobiography—information she later passed on to her great-grandchildren—how the various kinds of lighting devices marked the progression of her lifetime events. She was born by candlelight, was married by the light of a kerosine lamp, and finally had electricity installed in her home by having lines run through the gas pipes that had originally supplied gaslight to her family so that in each room a single bulb hung from the ceiling at the end of a wire. She ended her story with a paean of praise for the modern radio programs that made her old age so happy.

Now examine the suggested opening paragraph form above. It contains a number of elements that you will use over and over again as you begin your detective work on your ancestry. Note that it contains full names of the seven persons it mentions. No abbreviations are used. The father is not C. S. Peters; the husband is not J. S. Helms. The females are given their full names. Mrs. Charles Spencer Peters is Margaret (Dorman) Peters and Mrs. Bernard Carmichael Helms is Lorena (Sylvester) Helms. Too often, you will find that only the first name of females has been used in records, creating difficulties for any researcher later on. Note the form used for the dates: 10 April 1903, 5 July 1901. This is not an affectation employed by someone who was in the military during the late wars. It is done in genealogical recording so that there can be no confusion created by figures in juxtaposition— for instance, 10-4-03 or 10/4/03, which might mean 1803 or 1903. If, in the very beginning, this way of recording dates is adopted, a great deal of inaccuracy will be avoided, since 10 April 1903, or any other date so written, can never be confused.

There are, interestingly enough, many facts in that first paragraph of tremendous help to any future member of the family, even if the autobiography never gets beyond that one paragraph. It reveals that Shirley was the third child of her parents—that she had a sister and a brother older than she, placing her in the framework of a full complement of siblings. The paragraph also reveals that Shirley was born in Missouri to a Baptist family; that, as is the custom in that church, she was baptized when she was old enough to become a member; and that she married a man from California in a small town in Illinois.

Since the population of America has always been mobile, and since sons and daughters have been leaving home for so many different reasons and for so many years, there is an added complication in any genealogical study done in the United States. For this reason the importance of recording the whos, whens, and wheres of your family's history must be emphasized. A study of that suggested first paragraph reveals a concise way to record the answers to those questions. Later, as the pattern of your life is developed, the autobiography will hopefully continue to fill out the why and how.

However comprehensive that single opening paragraph, it does not fulfill one very important requirement. It does not give the *proof* for any of the statements it makes. Even though Shirley thinks that all the facts she has recorded are accurate (mostly because they were told to her by her parents and by her husband's parents), as the family genealogist she will have to collect proof for each statement. Birth certificates, baptismal certificates, marriage records, death records, cemetery or gravestone records—all these documents and many more should be accumulated to prove the statements made. Later we shall consider how to obtain this documentation and how to use it. As you will come to realize, documentation will be the backbone of your research.

Let us assume now that, like Shirley, you have plunged into your autobiography and have done all you want to on it at this time. You may not only have the facts of your own existence but have found proofs to substantiate them—birth or baptismal certificate and other legal documents—carefully stored away by your parents. You have reached an interesting point and are now ready to begin a new experience in searching.

With a fresh notebook and well-sharpened pencils it is now time for you to begin picking the brains of every relative and old friend of the family you can locate. It is advisable to start with the very oldest such person you know. An unobtrusive tape recorder is an excellent tool here, but many older people can be turned off by facing even a hidden microphone. In this situation he or she may not be cooperative, so talk it over before you decide to use the recording device. A truly considerate, courteous, and kindly approach will usually produce good answers to questions asked, especially if you do not give the impression that you are prying. When you start talking with a relative and begin to jot down the notes of the conversation, be sure to identify the informant on the top of the page and give the time and place of the interview so that you can accurately quote him or her as your source for statements you may want to use later. Identifying every source is important.

Not everything heard in interviews with relatives and old friends is going to be accurate. Sometimes you will find conflicting statements, but don't get into arguments. That is a sure way to close off valuable clues or information. Take voluminous notes during conversations, especially remembering that who, when, and where are the basic questions for which you want answers. Also get down as much of the what, how, and why as the person can supply. You will find that you will be told some stories about one person that may apply to another when you come to analyzing what you have heard. You may find the story twisted by time and an imperfect memory, but don't be bothered by that. This is all part of the sleuthing. Just remember to take good notes.

In one interview a searcher was told by an ancient second cousin of his father that his

10

great-grandfather "had been killed out west by an Iroquois Indian, while he was lying sick in bed with typhoid fever." The interviewer took the information just as it was given and asked, "Where out west was he killed?" The cousin didn't know the exact location, only that it was "out west." Later, after learning more about the family from other sources, the interviewer obtained a death record for the great-grandfather which showed that he had died of typhoid in Irondequoit, New York, a town many miles west of the place in which he had been born.

The most outrageous family traditions usually have a kernel of truth in them, and searching for that truth can be highly rewarding as well as revealing. One elderly maternal grandmother told a grandson who was tracing her line that it would be useless to try because her own paternal grandfather, whom she remembered well, couldn't speak English. He was, she said, German. Some years later, after further research on the family and more reading about the immigrants who had settled America, the interviewer discovered that his grandmother had been partially correct: her grandfather had *not* spoken English. But the probability was that he had been Dutch, not German, since he was descended from an old Dutch family that had settled in New Amsterdam (New York City) as early as 1640. (Perhaps someone had once confused "Dutch" with the German word *Deutsch*, meaning German.) Up until the early part of the nineteenth century many of these families used their native language while they were in their homes. Since the great-grandfather had died about 1860 when his granddaughter was a little girl, she remembered only that she could not communicate with him in her language. Her deduction that his line could not be traced turned out to be erroneous.

It is surprising how frequently interviews with family members give valuable leads to other relatives about whom no previous knowledge has existed. Many old family ties may be discovered in this way, the most rewarding occurring when similar interests and abilities are found in the "new" relative. For the seeker who feels isolated and alone in his search for identity, the roots will be far deeper and more pervasive than he had ever imagined.

A young man who grew up in the East on a farm in the backcountry decided that he would go into the city to earn his living, that farming was not for him. He had no difficulty finding a job within the first week of his stay in the city. But one of the questions asked of him over and over again was, "Are you of the [Blank] family?" At first the question puzzled him because he had no idea of his own heritage, but in the city his name was well known. Another person of that same name had been a founder of both the city and the colony, and he found that the name opened doors that would ordinarily have been closed to him. It was then that he began to look at local history to discover what kind of people he was descended from. He learned that they were good businessmen of high principles, and the probability was that, because he bore the same name, he was expected to emulate them. From this new knowledge he developed a simple pride. As he learned more and more about the family, he grew and prospered. In one sense this story is merely a variation on the theme of the self-fulfilling prophecy, but for this particular man an interest in his heritage turned out to be a very good thing.

Sometimes, through interviews with family members, memorabilia and heirlooms are found, often in the most unlikely places. Picture albums and portraits are uncovered in boxes of family papers stored in barn lofts or attics. Often there is no identification for the pictures or portraits—whoever knew the names is gone—but their location should be recorded in your notebook for future reference. Although their helpfulness may not be immediately apparent, as your skill in research develops you will find that the time will come when information so recorded may become a highly important clue.

One young man was told that his great-grandfather had been a clergyman. A pressed glass goblet with a grapevine and leaf design was treasured by the young man's mother and kept in the china closet in the dining room; she frequently described it as "the goblet used as a communion cup by your great-grandfather in the days before silver communion services." Since both his parents had died by the time the young man was ready to investigate his maternal line, he found that he had very little real information on which to base his search. All he really knew were the few stories his mother had told him. Yet nothing he discovered about his maternal great-grandfather supported his mother's belief that his occupation had ever been in the ministry. As it turned out, the man had been a carpenter and house builder. Entirely by accident, while reading a nineteenth-century short history of splinter religions that had developed in the area where his grandmother was born, the young man came upon the name of his great-grandfather, who, then a bachelor, had joined one of the communes and had been ordained their minister. Disenchantment and adverse economics had disbanded the group, and his great-grandfather had "returned to the world" bringing with him as a memento the pressed glass cup that had been used in the commune. The connection of the heirloom goblet and great-grandfather with a splinter religious sect and its community life had either been lost or never told to his children. The antique glass remained as mute evidence that led a descendant back to an era he found startlingly similar to the one he lived in, with its communes and different religious beliefs.

There is always the possibility that, through communication with family members, one of the greatest treasures, a Family Bible record, will be found. There may be only a rumor that one exists, but that rumor should be followed carefully and gently pursued to bring the searcher the full satisfaction of actually seeing the volume or any loose pages of records that may exist.

Sometimes this presents a problem. It is possible that the owner will consider anyone else's interest in the record as an invasion of privacy. There are even family members who will sit with arms wrapped around the Bible, clutching it, while saying, "No, it's mine. You can't have it." Patient explaining may bring such a relative to the point of allowing the book to be opened, but sometimes the effort is futile. On the other hand, there are many who are eager to share their treasure and who need no persuasion. Be very grateful that such people exist when you find them. One way to reciprocate is to share some of your family knowledge with them.

If the owner senses your concern for his papers and offers them to you, accept them thankfully and have copies made for him. Your own use of them will be limited to whatever information they supply, but as living memorials of the past they deserve a better fate than to be once again stored and "lost." Give some thought to the future of those papers and do what you can to have them deposited in your state library or state archives, or with a genealogical or historical society that has adequate facilities for their care.

When talking with relatives, it is always

advisable to inquire about any family papers that may have been tucked away—single pieces that may not have been put into the box and stored in attic or barn. Keep looking for diaries, letters, military discharges, baptismal certificates, fraternity or club membership certificates, and those hordes of newspaper clippings someone took time to collect, but too often forgot to identify and date. Diaries were usually not the line-a-day type, but were depositories for thoughts and reactions to events. They are valuable because they are the personal expressions of the life we are trying to reconstruct. Letters were not hastily typed notes, but usually contained news from home or from faraway family members. Since they were not frequent, letters were treasured. Those from men in military service were especially important to the folks back home and are of the greatest value in filling out details of the events and period they describe. Membership certificates in fraternal organizations reveal another facet of a person's life if, like other papers, they can be found. Finding them is often a problem, but sometimes a fortuitous accident can help, as happened in the following case.

A searcher was having great difficulty in

identifying the wife of one of his ancestors, his only clue being that her maiden name was Roxanney Brown. The problem seemed insoluble until one day when he was admiring a comic watercolor hanging on the wall in his cousin's house. The cousin lifted the painting from the hook to look for the name of the artist and accidentally dropped it. As the glass and frame smashed, they saw behind the watercolor an "In Memoriam" death notice and eulogy, printed on a handpress on newsprint. It gave the names of Roxanney's parents, her birthplace and date, whom she had married and when, and her death date. The little handbill revealed that Roxanney had been a very religious woman who had put off her own baptism hoping that her husband would consent to join her, but he never got around to it. Thus the handbill also explained why the searcher had been unable to find an early baptismal date for Roxanney's husband, William.

There are some families, of course, who have the reputation of never keeping anything, but even these families, when gently pressed, can produce some forgotten piece that can be helpful. Often these are found tucked into books or Bibles, hidden in bureau drawers, lying in shoe boxes or hatboxes, or pasted into scrapbooks along with recipes, bills, postcards, jokes, and pictures. Marriage certificates were so cherished by some wives that they were framed and hung over the bed, where they remained until both the original occupants had no further need of the bed. Then someone put away the certificates, now faded and crisp with age, and forgot them until the picture frames seemed quaint and reusable.

Perhaps you are one of those who have waited too long to build a family history. The people who could have answered many of your questions have long since departed this world, or their residences are no longer known to you. But it is not a hopeless task, even though you don't have a verbal record from those who were contemporary with your parents or grandparents. Your approach to the family is the same: start with yourself. In writing an autobiography, no matter how brief, you may well find that the doors of your memory open to let loose a flood of data about relatives you have long since forgotten. "Why, I haven't thought about Great-uncle George in years! He was Grandma's 'baby brother,' as she used to call him, and Great-aunt Mary was Grandma's 'big sister'!" There you have clues to your family line, coming from memories released by your effort to reconstruct your own life. It will surprise you to discover how much will come back to you once you let yourself remember. Being the middle finger in the hand, or the link between generations, can be very rewarding when you learn what a depository your memory is. If you are a late starter, your rememberings should be jotted in your notebook, just as though they were from interviews with relatives. They may be some of the most important clues you will find.

If your family came to America in the last century, there is no need to feel that tracing it is impossible or even unworthy of your time. You are probably not the last descendant of those immigants. The autobiography you write may become valuable source material for other descendants and researchers. The data you collect from relatives in this country, the stories you were told of events "back home" in the "old country," all the basic genealogical information you can piece together, will give you a sense of belonging to a wonderful group of people—your family—whose feet have been placed firmly in a new world, but whose roots go back into another. In America we are all descendants of immigrants, whether early or late arrivals. Each of us belongs to a unique, special family. The records of the latecomers are valuable and should be preserved for the oncoming generations, just as the earlier arrivals attempted to preserve their history for their descendants.

2

Keeping Records

As you talk and correspond with relatives, and as you later begin research in other sources, the volume of material for your family history will grow. As in any hobby or business, the stock must be kept in order. In genealogy the accumulation divides into at least three categories: (1) the main body of information; (2) the documentation to prove its accuracy; and (3) illustrations such as pictures of places, people, and things, or maps, all of which can be used to enhance the finished product.

Keeping the records organized and readily available need not be complicated. There is no set standard form. The only criterion for the system you inaugurate is that it be readily understandable to you or anyone else who uses it.

Elaborate systems have been developed and printed forms are available for all aspects of genealogical research. If you are one who

FAMILY GROUP SHEET

HUSBAND _____

Born _____ Place _____
Chr. _____ Place _____
Marr. _____ Place _____
Died _____ Place _____
Bur. _____ Place _____

HUSBAND'S FATHER _____ **HUSBAND'S MOTHER** _____

HUSBAND'S OTHER WIVES _____

WIFE _____

Born _____ Place _____
Chr. _____ Place _____
Died _____ Place _____
Bur. _____ Place _____

WIFE'S FATHER _____ **WIFE'S MOTHER** _____

WIFE'S OTHER HUSBANDS _____

CHILDREN		SEX	WHEN AND WHERE BORN				WHEN DIED		
Surname	Given names	M/F	Day Month Year	Town	County	State or Country	Day	Month	Year
1									
2									
3									
4									
5									

SOURCES OF INFORMATION

OTHER MARRIAGES

Date of First Marriage   To Whom

23

likes an elaborate bookkeeping system, you will probably be delighted with the great variety of printed forms offered for sale to the genealogist. Usually, though, the average family researcher finds simple recording devices sufficient. You are entirely free to set up a system that meets your own needs, as long as it's a system that can grow with you.

You started your family research with yourself. Now, as it progresses generation by generation backward from you to your parents and then to their parents, and as you reach back for the earliest account you can find, it will build. The simplest method for recording this information is in your permanent notebook. Head the first sheet —the one where you have recorded the data about yourself—with your name. Then start a page for the parent whose line you have selected to trace first, and pages for each generation, progressing backward. This sets up a basic system for transferring data as you collect them. Additional pages of all kinds can be added. This same simple system can be worked with large file cards, if you prefer them to notebooks.

Supplemental forms, such as the Family Group Sheet (see preceding page), can be

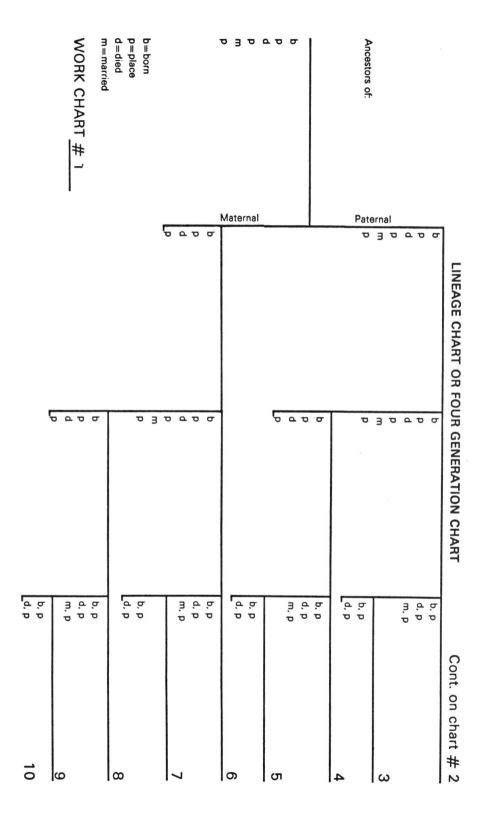

LINEAGE CHART OR FOUR GENERATION CHART

Cont. on chart # 2

Ancestors of:

b
p
d
p
m
p

Paternal

b
d
p
m
p
p

Maternal

b
p
d
p
p

b
p
m
p
d
p
b
p

b
p
d
p
b

b
p
m
p
d
p
b

b, p
d, p
m, p

3

b, p
d, p

4

b, p
d, p
m, p

5

b, p
d, p

6

m, p
d, p
b, p

7

d, p
d, p
b, p

8

b, p
d, p
m, p

9

b, p
d, p

10

b=born
p=place
d=died
m=married

p=place
d=died
m=married
b=born

WORK CHART # 1

25

inserted for each generation. This brings the parents and their children together on one page for reference. It also quickly shows just exactly where you need to seek out material you lack. The Family Group Record will not be proof of the data recorded, but it does provide limited space for a reference as to where the information was found. And this is an important part: always record on the basic notebook page or card the full reference for documentation of each item.

It is also helpful, when working on a single line, to keep a simple Lineage Chart or Four Generation Chart. (See preceding page.) This shows at a glance the work progress and also enables you to spot the missing data more quickly.

If you are bravely tackling more than one line at a time, there is a Nine or Ten Generation Lineage Chart that has a different purpose from the simpler chart. This larger chart is cumulative, designed to record up to 256 direct ancestors. It is useful when you have completed research on a number of lines, or even while your work is in progress. For the first three or four generations of each family line, the chart has places for entering births, marriages, and deaths. Then, as the number of lines increases with each generation, there is room on the chart only for the names of husbands and wives. This larger chart does offer, however, a simple numbering system. You may want to use it in your notebook for ready reference as you develop more than one line. These charts can be carried in the front of your permanent record book, since they fold down to notebook size.

Here are some rules of thumb that are helpful no matter which recording system you use:

1. When entering data that has not been documented, use a pencil. The item may be erased and entered in ink when you have proof.

2. Always use full, complete names, especially of persons and places. If someone has been known by a nickname, use the full proper name first, followed by the nickname in parentheses: Michael John (Patsy) Borgos. In the case of places, if a county is given be sure to record it as well: Freehold, Monmouth County, New Jersey.

3. It is often helpful, when exact or even approximate dates are not given, to try to figure them out through deduction. Entered in pencil, with parentheses around them, they are a guide to the era in which

research needs to be done. For example, if you know a marriage date and want to know when the husband was born, subtract twenty-five years to reach his probable birth date (if it was a first marriage). For the wife, subtract twenty-one years.

William Short married Maria Pierce 11 November 1857. William Short was born (c. 1832); Maria born (c. 1836)

4. If you know the birth date of the first child, subtract twenty-six years for the husband's birth date and twenty-two years for the wife's. (These rules of deduction are based on the fact that a generation is usually considered to be about thirty years.)

5. Birth dates of children usually occur in some kind of pattern. Sometimes a child is born every eighteen months, or every two, or even three, years. By the same token, if there is a large gap found between children's birth dates, it can sometimes indicate one of a number of things—an unrecorded child, a stillborn child, a divorce, the death of a wife and a remarriage, or a father who is away for service at sea or in the army, or who is pioneering to find a suitable

new home, or perhaps even away in the gold rush.

The Hodkins family had a son, George, born in 1888 and a daughter, Ruth, born in 1892. In 1896 an unnamed boy died at birth. In 1900 a son named Harry was born. Family records—in this case, letters —showed that there was a girl named Helen, whose birth was not recorded in civil records. The last child, whose name was Margaret, was born in 1908. Looking at the pattern of childbearing in this particular family (with the exception of 1904, a child every four years) and also at the fact that Helen had told her own children about her position among her siblings, suggests that she was probably born in 1904. In any case, despite the lack of documentation, both her gravestone and her official death record carried the 1904 date.

In the Marks family Bible the birth of children was given as follows: George Borden Marks born 1808; Ruth Ellen Marks born 1810; Herbert John Marks born 1812; Sylvia Ann Marks born 1816; Augustus Simon Marks born 1819; Jonathan Henry Marks born 1822. In this family, with a child every two years, the hiatus between 1812 and 1816, and a three-year period between subsequent children, was later proved to result from the death of the first wife, a second marriage, and a new pattern of childbearing—in this case children coming less frequently.

There are some instances of a man's being married to more than one woman (at different times) with the same first name. In one case, the children by the first wife came at regular intervals. When the first wife died and the husband married again, the intervals between children were found to be longer—three years instead of two. The difference in the frequency of childbearing does not necessarily mean that there have been two wives with the same name, but a change of periods between children does lead the searcher to suspect a second marriage if it is not already known.

6. Adopted children cannot claim lineal descent from the adopting family and can only try to prove their descent through their natural parents' lines. If a child is known to be adopted, that fact should be indicated by writing either "A" or "adopted" on the record. This is very important for genealogical reasons, since it is documented bloodlines that determine a family's lineage. An

adoption is considered family *history*, not lineage.

A retired gentleman who wanted his family history done was very cooperative about giving the researcher all the data he had left from his family after their homestead had burned. From his memory he was able to supply dates and places for his immediate household. This gentleman had served in the U.S. Navy during World War I. Stationed in New York City for a while before his honorable discharge, he courted a girl from his hometown, but he had no remembrance of their ever having been married. The girl claimed that they had been married in Elkton, Maryland, on one of his weekend leaves. The gentleman had never checked the records or seen a marriage certificate, but accepted the statement from the girl that they were then man and wife. The young wife moved into the home of the gentleman's parents until they could find a home of their own, and a boy was born about nine months after the alleged marriage. After the baby was born, the young wife left her husband and disappeared. The young man, who was still living with his parents, accepted the child as his own and raised him, with his parents' help. The boy grew up, married, and had

31

two sons. All this was recorded in the family history, but after it was completed, the gentleman died. His death notice, which was in the newspaper, was seen by his runaway wife, the son's mother. She went to his funeral incognito, as a former friend, for of course her son would not recognize her. After the old gentleman was buried, the son received a letter from his mother, who finally told him the truth: he was the son of another man; his "father" had known this and had adopted him, but had said nothing to his own parents in order not to disturb their happiness in having a grandson. No record of the marriage in Elkton had ever been discovered by the researcher, of course, and the circumstances as stated to the searcher by the gentleman-"father" had given no hint of the true story. The family history stands as written, untruthfully giving the illegitimate, but adopted, boy a full family line which is not rightfully his. Had the story been known, the finished line would have ended with the "father" or would have carried the story of the adopted son with an "A" to indicate the truth.

7. If there is a stillborn child, include the fact, giving the name if any, or the sex if known.

8. Before a date is entered, don't forget to use the acceptable order—date, month, year: 12 October 1863. Check its accuracy. Is it plausible? Does it fall within a believable period? Were the parents at proper childbearing ages when all the children attributed to them were born? (Childbearing years for women are usually age thirteen to forty-eight, later for men.) Are the birth dates of the children all before the death of either of the parents? Or are they within nine months of the death of the father? Do the time and places in which the children were born correspond with the known time and places of residence of the parents?

For example, the following paragraph is quoted from a letter:

John Silver was born 8 May 1812 and died intestate 27 September 1843. He married first, 4 June 1833, Ellen Marple born 5 August 1812, who died 7 January 1841. He married second, 14 June 1841, widow Susan Winne who died 2 February 1878 in her 68th year. John's children were: Jane born 16 April 1834; Ellen born 14 June 1837; John Jr. born about 1841; Peter Silver born 26 December 1841; Eleanor born 4 September 1842 and Nathan born 1 October 1843.

Even a quick reading through these data makes us realize there is something here that isn't quite clear. Looking at the facts as given more carefully, we find a not unusual picture of family life and problems. We must test the plausibility of some of this information with simple arithmetic: John and Ellen were both young, about twenty-one years old, when they married. Their first daughter, Jane, arrived less than a year later. When we note that Ellen arrived three years later, and a son, John, not for four more years, we begin to suspect that there were some stillborn children between the three who lived, especially since no firm date of birth is found for the son John, Jr., "born about 1841." Ellen died in January 1841, leading us to conjecture that the birth of John, Jr., may have been a contributing cause of the mother's death, as she was only twenty-nine years old. Within six months John, Sr., was remarried, a normal enough circumstance for a young widower who has been left with two girls, ages seven and four, and a newborn son. Six months after the second marriage there was another son, Peter; then ten months later a daughter, Eleanor. Four days after the father died, a posthumous son, Nathan, came along. Once more Susan was widowed, but now she had six Silver children dependent on her. Later, it was discovered from Susan's will that she had two children by her first husband who had gone to live in the Silver home when she married John, Sr., so that actually, there were eight small children from newborn to age nine years needing her care. Just to put down a series of dates without stopping to analyze them is not enough. The picture emerges only when we consider carefully the plausibility of what we have found.

9. Wherever you are searching and taking notes, always remember to put on the top line of your notebook page the name of the place and the date on which the searching is being done. Whatever you find, be sure to put down the book, page or document number, and the date—i.e., the full identification of the source used. Sometimes, in the excitement occasioned by a real "find," it's easy to forget to record the complete source, but when this happens it can cause real problems later.

10. Some researchers like to keep a dated cumulative list of the libraries, courthouses,

cemeteries, and other places they visit. This can be very helpful, since it can eliminate a source you are reconsidering or even remind you of forgotten data you had already collected. It is also recommended that a list of sources be developed for the area in which a family lived. This can be checked off as you complete research on an individual, specific family. Later you may have to go back to those listed sources because you may have discovered elsewhere who the great-grandfather was. Simple devices such as these can save a great deal of time, yet often people fail to take the time to develop them. One nice little elderly lady who fancied herself as a genealogist did her research in only one library with a good genealogy collection. She had never learned how to do research or keep records, but kept her jottings on all sizes and shapes of scrap paper. It became a sad joke among other more enlightened searchers that Miss S. had gone back to the same book of published records five or six times in a day of research. This was a habit with her. She kept no record of what she had already consulted, and it was pathetic to see her shake her head woefully and to hear her whisper, "It should be in there, but I can't find it. Oh, dear."

11. When you take extracts from records, it is well first to identify the source, then copy the extract exactly as it is written. Interpretation of it can come later, when you have time to study the verbatim copy you have made. Names especially should be copied just as found, although the spelling may not agree with the present way the name is spelled. Even so simple a name as Mott has been found with half a dozen spellings or more: Mot, Mots, Motte, Mote, Moat, Mothe, deMoth, etc. A name such as Cashaw can turn up with as many different variations: Chassouw, Cusshaw, Casou, Corsiou, Corsyou, Cessouw, Kersiou, Kershou, and Kershow.

12. A simple way to keep records is to keep a separate page or pages in your notebook for each person being researched. Bring together on this record page all the various items found concerning this person, with their source. Eventually you will find, when you come to write a biographical sketch, that you already have a chronological order you can use to follow this individual through life (all with the necessary documentation):

June 1906: Graduated from Lexington High School (Year Book)

September 1906: Entered Lane Business College and

June 1910: Graduated (college Year Book)

15 July 1910: Married Hazel Bond (wedding certificate)

1910–1912: Rented house at 12 Sims Street (lease)

3 February 1912: Bought house at 34 Junio Street (deed)
"he paid all cash, using the money grandfather had left him" (Uncle Peter's statement, 6 March 1965)

7 February 1912: First child, John, born in new house (Bible record)

3 August 1913: Left Smith Brothers, where he was an accountant, to open his own office at 743 Fifth Street (Uncle Peter, 6 March 1965)

7 June 1914: Daughter Elizabeth was born (Bible record)

1 December 1915: Closed office and went to work at Butlers Department Store as head of credit department (*Butlers Bugle*, 15 December 1915)

1917–1919: Headed Liberty Loan drives in Butlers Store that were oversubscribed (*News Herald* clippings 10 May and 17 October 1917, 15 June and 21 October 1918)

1920: Elected Deacon at First Presbyterian Church (church record)

1923: Elder at the church (church record)

1926: Chairman of Finance Committee at church (church record)

1928: Treasurer of Butlers Department Store (*News Herald* clipping, 1 August 1928)

1929: Member of Town Ways and Means Committee (*News Herald* clipping, 23 October 1929)

13. The documentation in this particular example brings up the next rule of thumb. Your documentation may consist of the originals of certificates, deeds, wills, military service records, family papers, and newspaper clippings. They need special treatment since they are your proofs, all of which are subject to destruction if not properly preserved. It is best to have all such items copied. The copy can then be used while the work is in progress. The original should be safely stored in a Book of Evidence. A large ring binder equipped with transparent Mylar double pages will keep all such basic items clean and free from the hazards of handling. All originals pertaining to one family can be kept together, each in

its separate Mylar enclosure. These may include identified pictures, school certificates —whatever you have been using for proof of statements. Another advantage is that a Book of Evidence will relieve you of the necessity of carrying so much with you on a research trip. And, finally, it will keep the material clean for inclusion in your finished work. If sections of evidence become too large, they can be removed from the notebook in their protective Mylar covers to a vertical file. Since legal documents should not be kept folded, making copies of them and then covering and placing them in a file is one way to preserve them for those who come after.

The ideal way to study any document is to have the original available for ready reference. The next best way is to make a photocopy so that it may be studied in the quiet of your own home where you can work on it at your leisure. But to simplify the research process, it may be expedient to resort to the time-honored processes of abstracting, excerpting, extracting, or transcribing records. These methods have been called genealogical shorthand. They are described in this next section.

There is a difference among the four methods of making useful genealogical notes. Each has something to recommend it, and each is useful in solving problems. They are most useful when working with lengthy public records, printed genealogies, genealogical publications, histories, census records, military and pension records, etc. Whichever method you choose, be sure to note where you acquired the information, along with the place and date on which it was found.

Transcribing is making a copy of a record, exactly as the record is found. This is best accomplished by photocopy, but if you must, do it yourself by typing or longhand. Any unusual spellings, sentence structure, or word uses should be underlined or marked [sic], meaning "just so." When you next consult your transcription, you will then be sure that you didn't copy something incorrectly. If you possibly can, have someone proofread your transcript while the original is before both of you. You will find that an accurate transcription is an absolute must if you plan to print your family history, since most editors will not transcribe public documents for your book, even from photocopy. They will use good copies for illustrations, as they will pictures, but if the total record is to appear in the text, you must transcribe it.

Abstracting may serve your purpose when you have material that is valuable to you, either historical or genealogical. Abstracting consists of making a summary of the important data. You can do this as an outline such as you would in abstracting a deed, noting all the important and necessary inclusions. Abstracting may be done in sentence form (as long as you are sure to include all the necessary information) by running it in consecutive sentences or phrases.

Extracting is the process of taking from a record only the pertinent material needed for your specific problem. Suppose you were looking for the name of the wife of a man who was selling some of his property in 1872. Your extract of that deed would read:

Deed of 25 May 1872: John Miller of Middletown, S.C. Also signed by wife Mary L. Miller

Here the middle initial was needed to help identify John's wife; the L. was the clue to her maiden name, Lane. If a will were being searched for the name of the surviving wife and children, you would need to extract only that portion:

Will of June 1877: John Miller names "my present wife" Jane B. Miller; my son John L. Miller . . . daughter Mary Miller . . . son Jerome B. Miller, when they are of age.

This gives the clues that John Miller had a second wife named Jane B. and that all the children were minors.

Excerpting is the process of taking from a record the actual wording of a sentence or apropos phrase to fulfill some requirement or lack in your notes:

Deed of 25 May 1872: John Miller of Middletown, S.C. to Peter White, names the bounds of his woodlot "bounded east by the homelot of James Lane, deceased."

In excerpting, the phrase or sentence should be copied in quotes, spelling all the words exactly as found in the original and quoting numerals exactly as written. Even if you believe them to be inaccurate, don't change name spellings in any excerpt. Underlining the phrase you need calls it to your attention when you refer to your notes.

There is no one system of genealogical shorthand that is better to use than any other in taking notes. It is for you to decide the value of the information you find in your conversations, correspondence, and records. Use whatever method comes easiest to you and gives you the most pertinent data. By experimentation you will soon develop your own most convenient methods of taking notes and recording data.

3

Using Libraries

Collecting information from the family through conversations and correspondence is a continuing process that can often go on for years. The recording of the body of information shows that research must be undertaken to fill some of the gaps. To locate a generation geographically and learn its vital statistics are not enough. The generations must be reconstructed in their own period of history, clothed in the mental and physical garments they wore, reconstituted as part of their environment. This is what good genealogy does: it locates births, marriages and deaths, then adds pertinent biographical details. For this kind of thorough research the library is one of the best places to work. Libraries are most useful at the beginning of research and then much later when exploration of other sources has turned up additional clues.

There was a time not too long ago when

most librarians had a dim view of the amateur genealogist. Genealogy—even the mention of it—had a way of inspiring their cynicism, but perhaps they were justified. Would-be family historians and genealogists, possibly for the first time in their lives, were entering the very special world of research with its high standards of scholarship. They were lost and confused in a place where librarians and skilled researchers were so much at home. It is still possible to meet librarians who are short tempered or annoyed with the beginning researcher, but if a family historian will go into the library with the proper attitude, this may be overcome.

As well as genealogical sections in local libraries, there are increasing numbers of libraries that are devoted entirely to genealogy. The status of genealogy is no longer that of a lesser servant to history. Genealogy and history are now recognized as inseparable. The historian deals with masses of people and massive events, while the genealogist is specific about a person in the mass affected by the massive events. Through information found in personal letters, diaries, and minutiae discovered in family searches, the genealogist becomes a historian, contributing new knowledge to the history field.

Genealogical collections are found in local libraries, county and state libraries, and special genealogical libraries. Their holdings differ widely, depending on the policies and objectives of the individual library and the funds available to purchase, maintain, and administer genealogical materials. In some places the genealogical sources are found in the history area; in others, in the socioeconomic division. In increasing frequency, they are located in a genealogy section. Often, the collections of local historical and genealogical societies that have no buildings of their own are deposited with the local or state library or in a college library.

On the first visit to any library for genealogical research it is usually wise to talk to the person in charge about the way the library is arranged and about the catalog or catalogs maintained. There is no need to go into a long, involved story about your family and your problem. The librarian or volunteer is not there to listen to why you are seeking information. The person in charge is there only to see that you are provided with books or other research material the library has that you need, or to help you find what isn't plainly in view on the open shelves.

Obviously, the place to start is with the

catalog. No two libraries will have the same type of catalog. Each has its own system, some antedating the formation of presently acceptable library principles and practices. One library in the New York area, founded in the mid-nineteenth century, has a general catalog that is similar to a shelf list, but its genealogical materials are cataloged in numerous separate files: Biography, Families, Geographical, Manuscript, Bible and Family Records, Newspapers, Microcard and Microfilm. This has been done to aid the family and local historians who are the predominant users of this historical library. Unfortunately, the materials have never been cataloged by any system. In direct contrast is any modern library using the Library of Congress cataloging system in which every book is numbered and cross reference cards make it easy to locate materials on numbered shelves. There are many libraries that fall between these two extremes, in having a general catalog of the total library and a separate one in the history or genealogy area. Get to know the library through its catalogs so you can decide how it can best serve you.

Among the materials you will be seeking first are local histories of the area in which your first problem lies. There was a period around our national Centennial in 1876 when people began to realize that it had been a century since we became a nation and few people had compiled histories of what had happened locally. The result was a rash of state, county, and town histories in which an attempt was made to fill the gap. Some of the resulting histories are excellent, but most are undocumented. They usually contain information concerning the churches, along with the earliest and later settlers and where they came from. Many of these histories contain biographies of local persons, in which it is possible to pick up useful clues. These historical accounts serve the purpose of giving a great deal of pertinent data that it is important not to overlook, for a thorough acquaintance with the area in which you are seeking records is essential. Its history will form the background into which you will fit the lives of the people you are trying to find. In some towns and cities there has been interest in local history for the past century and, with the Bicentennial, interest in collecting and publishing local information was again aroused. None of these collections and publications should be bypassed, for they are often the result of careful research in data undiscovered and unknown in the nineteenth century. Some of it is based on genealogical collections that were made in that period.

Genealogies have been written of hundreds of families and of probably as many single family lines. If the library has genealogies with your family name, be sure to examine all of them. It can, and often does, happen that having obtained sufficient information on your own family, you can now latch on to the rest of the line in a previously compiled genealogy. A warning word, however: formerly, genealogists did not document their work. They talked and corresponded with people who gave them information and even sent them family and Bible records, but no acknowledgment was made of the source. Many of the data are based on lost documents and on letters that have been destroyed. If the author has not given proof for his statements, the printed genealogy or the manuscript should be regarded as presenting only *clues*. You must do what the author failed to do: find the proof. Just because a family line is printed or is in manuscript form deposited in a library does not make the data accurate. Perhaps the author wrote that he had found the dates he used in a "Family Record" or "Family Bible" but did not give the location of either. This is often frustrating, but it gives the searcher hope that such a record may exist some place or that its equivalent may be located in another set of records.

In working with printed or typed genealogical material in libraries, you will often find that, despite library rules prohibiting writing in books or defacing them in other ways, someone who has used the book before you has written in statements or dates that correct the text. These do not constitute proof either. If you wish to add these penciled notes to your own, you may do so, but they will also serve only as *clues*—in this case signifying that someone else may have found something that the author had not known about. If you have found information that disagrees with what you find printed or typed in the library's books, it is hoped that you will conform to the library's regulations. Give the information you have found, with its source, to the person in charge. Usually corrections are welcomed and are typed by the librarian on a piece of paper and pasted into the reference book with your name as the donor. Some older genealogies will be found to have several of these corrections, which, because their source is given, can be checked. Anything just jotted into a book, without a source, could be as incorrect as the original text may have been. This is a tricky little bit of byplay that occurs not only in genealogies, but in almost every kind of reference work. It is a great nuisance to the researcher as well as an annoyance to the library if a correction is not made in the correct manner.

One fine source that is being found in more and more libraries is the work of local people who realize the value of their records to the family historian and genealogist (as well as to the historian). These dedicated folk are doing a tremendous job in every section of the country. For some of their work they find funds available for publishing, but whether it ever gets into print, their contributions are priceless. They collect and copy cemetery inscriptions, church records, and old family records; interview old people; and prepare indexes of administrations, wills, and land and town records. Some spend long and interesting hours culling vital records from local newspapers, which they type on catalog cards or prepare as typed indexed lists. A library with deposits of these local resources can be of paramount importance to the genealogist. They may provide the preliminary information you need before you invade county clerks' offices and county courthouses.

Often overlooked, but of great help, are the periodicals published by genealogical societies at home and abroad. They are equivalent to the trade newspapers and magazines so necessary to the intelligent businessman. In fact, they are the trade magazines of the family researcher. For many decades a number of genealogical periodicals have been devoted to the publication of records of families, churches, cemeteries, and towns, and to articles written on all phases of research. Full genealogies, usually indexed, have been published by some of the older magazines in installments running through many issues. They are an important tool, and complete sets of them are found in most genealogical collections.

In every state there is at least one designated library that receives each year a bound copy of all the records collected in that state by the many chapters of the Daughters of the American Revolution (the DAR). In some states the DAR work has resulted in hundreds of volumes of cemetery, church, family, and public records which are not available elsewhere. Collections from every state are also found in the DAR Library in

Washington, D.C., where they are brought together under one roof for reference. This library and the library of the Genealogical Society of the Church of Jesus Christ of Latter-day Saints in Salt Lake City are only two of several libraries with large and extensive collections from all over the United States. You may want to visit them.

Some libraries maintain a list of researchers who use their facilities, with the names of the families on which the searcher is working. This is a valuable source for anyone who wants to enter into correspondence with others who are working on the same family. Usually the other person has information you need, and vice versa, so that a good exchange can be made.

Among the sources that are good to consult in libraries will be maps, atlases, military records, professional and trade histories, and published lodge, club, and college records and lists. As you get farther into your research, you will find that libraries—depending on their age, size, and financial status —have anticipated the needs of historians and genealogists. Learning about their holdings through catalogs and digging into what they store form a large part of the pleasure of pursuing your family line. It is easy to be sidetracked—in fact, you may find yourself becoming a very knowledgeable local historian—but that is one of the pluses in genealogy!

4

Utilizing Geography and History

Since genealogy is the process of forming assumptions that must be tested to determine their accuracy, we cannot overlook any of the disciplines that can be useful. Geography and history are two that will help us project into the time and place in which a generation of a family lived out their lives. Having used family resources and found helpful library collections, we must come now to the study of a period in one particular place, and find the family in it, to answer our "When?" and "Where?" If we are lucky, perhaps even our "Why?" and "How?" will be answered. Geography and history go hand in hand at this point. Through reading about one we discover the other.

America was primarily settled from the east by peoples who left their homelands for different reasons to sail west. Their first settlements lay along the shores, clustered around good harbors or strung along rivers and streams. Waterways were their first lanes of communication and were also used to transport produce to larger settlements around good harbors. Rivers and streams supplied settlers with food by watering the bottomlands for planting and the meadows for salt hay so necessary to feed the colonists' cattle. And the water provided power to run their mills.

The geography of America has determined her local history in each phase of migration and development. As Indian paths across the first mountain barrier were followed westward, first in the search for better furs, then for better land, the men who dared to leave the comparative comforts of life in the increasingly crowded coastal areas were busy surviving and carving out a new life for themselves.

A certain amount of general history is linked with all phases of settlement and development of the country, but some of our states have shorter histories than others. The thirteen colonies became thirteen states by 1800, but from 1803, when Ohio entered statehood, until Hawaii became a state in 1959, there were others that came into the Union having little or no colonial history.

The problem of finding vital records for

an individual is not easily solved without a background knowledge of the history and geography of the area to be searched. The first step is to equip yourself with a good modern local map that will serve to orient you and aid in your further understanding of the information you obtain from older maps of the place and period being researched. From map study you will come to see the physical factors inherent in the land that helped to shape the lives of its inhabitants.

Maps showing the locale can be found in the library. They will give locations of settlements, towns, and even farms in relation to each other. Some towns were great distances apart. Others—villages, hamlets, or settlements—clustered around a mill or a trading post. The closeness of a town to a county border line may have a bearing on where research should be undertaken, for county lines were often changed and at times were even run through the center of a homestead. This will necessitate a search for records in more than one county.

A topographical map—that is, one that shows the geographical features of an area —should be helpful because rivers, mountains, marshes, and valleys all affected the lives of settlers and migrants. Old roads that seem rambling and unnecessarily curvaceous today were laid out along Indian trails or were carved through woodland and meadows, skirting great trees, rock outcroppings, or marshy areas, or sidestepping a homestead already established.

Mountains were barriers to settlement for a long time, although the dense forests that covered them supplied the colonists with wood for buildings and furniture, for heating, and later for commercial purposes.

In the valleys between protecting mountains and hills or along valley streams were found the best farmlands. How settlers cleared those hills and valleys of woodland for grazing and cultivation, and how the settlements, towns, and cities grew, all contributed to early local history.

The contour map—or a map with lines indicating the elevations of an area—will show the mountains that harbored wild animals and displaced Indians, mountains that would later yield coal and metals. The Appalachian Mountains formed a barrier that affected local history and genealogy enormously. Until it was safe to cross them in search of better land and greater security, they kept young men from seeking wives.

After a long day in the fields, lumbering in the foothills or working at a trade, a man would hardly want to climb over a mountain into the next valley to court. Instead, he sought eligible girls at the nearest farm. He traveled along a dirt road or a path through the woods, or took to his boat on the near-by stream. If by stream, he was likely to go upriver in the early evening because, by the end of a long day and an evening spent visiting, going downriver was easier. Court-ing time could not be wasted by climbing over a mountain and returning when the night animals were prowling, or by sailing too far. Where terrain interfered, propin-quity played a large role in courtship and marriage.

Local area maps will show how the set-tlers traveled, as well as where they may have attended church, paid taxes, and regis-tered their lands. When people moved, they rarely struck off tangentially unto unmarked territory. Usually they followed the blazed paths, even when migrating. It is important for you to know these paths when you are tracing where a family may have gone after they sold their property.

As the general history of an area was often affected by the geography of the land, so were the social and economic history. Lives of the farmers on the shallow topsoil of Vermont were entirely different from the lives of farmers on the alluvial soil of the deltas. The environment and the land on which they lived produced men with different attitudes, religious beliefs, and economic stability. Local history helps you to understand the details of the lives of the people—how they moved within their chosen area or why they migrated from or to it.

When the great westward push began after the Revolution, groups of people traveled over trails set by explorers. Some of these people were sufficiently strong and well supplied to travel far beyond the mountains. Others stopped along the way and settled in, creating new towns that then grew into cities. The history of the migration paths and the places migrants settled must be understood by even the beginning family historian, especially when he finds that the ancestor has "gone west."

Both local and national history are concerned with the labor force in every part of the land; this is naturally true, since men tend to live where there is work. Furthermore, the economic factors of life in a particular place have an effect on the lives of these men's families and their customs. When new industries move into an area, the population increases. When work is no longer available, families move out. This has been true throughout history. Where people go can become a genealogical research problem of no mean proportions, but the history of the area they left can often point the searcher in the right direction.

If work is constant or farming is productive and provides economic security, families may remain in one place for generations. Without a large influx of new families, local customs are maintained for a long time and are even strengthened. The families begin to form a cohesive group, the best example being the Amish in Pennsylvania. Local history helps to point out the nationality of the groups that settle there. These people bring with them from their homelands their customs in marriage, their religious faith, their total way of life. Sometimes, when great numbers of them congregate in one area, the original settlers' families would find it profitable to sell out to the newcomers and move on. Knowing the occupation of those who move may be helpful in tracing where they went, for work available in newly opened places often called out a family in which the father and older sons were skilled carpenters, blacksmiths, weavers, fishermen, or traders. Just as the earliest colonization of what is now the United States was accomplished by groups consisting of skilled workmen, so other settlements have needed and attracted the experienced worker. We are seeing this now in the growth and expansion of Alaska. In more modern times carloads of immigrants have been shipped out of the ports of entry directly to the farms and industries where they were needed. The mines of Pennsylvania and other Eastern states, the wheatlands in mid-America, the lumbering operations in the tall timberlands have all accepted and absorbed migrants, just as did various parts of the country when the railroads and canals were being built.

Wars have always had the effect of showing the men who fought them new and more desirable lands and ways of life. Our French and Indian Wars took men from their occupations and farms into militia companies that were formed to protect their homes, and also took some of those companies to distant areas they had only vaguely heard of. In the Revolutionary War men from all the colonies were moved about, some of them going away from home for the first time. These men did not return home and forget the lands and people they had seen. The Mexican War, the Civil War, and World Wars I and II had the same effect. To trace men and their families following a war may be difficult, but if the former soldier received either land or a pension for his services and moved on, he can probably be found in records in the part of the country where he served.

With changing times came changing names for many towns and counties. Gazetteers are excellent sources for tracing some of these changes. Some names of Indian origin were shortened or even eliminated. Rahway, New Jersey, was originally found as Rahawackbacka, Rahawack, Rawake, Roway, Raway, and finally Rahway. Milltown, so named because a mill was there, may later have been named Adams, perhaps to honor an early president. New York City was variously named Manhatta, New Amsterdam, and New-York. Gazetteers have picked up many of the name changes and give them along with changes in boundaries of towns, counties, and even states.

PART TWO
How to Use Public Records

5

Private and Public Records

Every record ever made has (or had at one time) a specific purpose. Church records are made for ecclesiastical reasons; they are used by the church to report to its governing body how it is fulfilling its parish obligations. They record the church finances, give a tally of the membership, and list the number of baptisms and marriages performed and the number of members buried. Sometimes the private records that had been previously recorded in the family Bible were placed there so the members of the family would not forget the most important events in their lives—births, marriages, and deaths. Public records are made and maintained for governmental reasons, since births, deaths, marriages, and divorces are matters of public health. Tax records are compiled to assure equal taxation based on evaluation. Records of voters are maintained to safeguard the voting process, so that each qualified citizen is assured of one vote. Public records are maintained at every level of government from village to Federal government and are paid for with tax money supplied by the public. Like private and ecclesiastical records, they are valuable tools for the genealogist.

Official records kept in villages and towns are of a miscellaneous nature, very often prescribed by local law. Sometimes periodical transfers are made to county or state depositories for preservation purposes if required by law; in any event, birth, marriage, and death records are usually found there. Since state laws providing for the recording of vital records were not all passed and enforced at the same time, there is a great deal of diversity among them. Even *within* a state the recording of births, marriages, and deaths starts at varying times. In Massachusetts for instance, the Town Clerks have retained the vital records of their towns; but because of the destruction of some of the records and the various founding dates of towns, the earliest records begin at different times. In Pennsylvania the County Clerk may have birth records from 1893 to 1907, marriage records for 1775, death records for 1834, burials from 1852 to 1855 and 1893 to 1907, and civil court records from 1780. Some Pennsylvania towns have sent their birth and death records from 1906 to the Bureau of Vital Statistics at Harrisburg.

For research under these circumstances, it is necessary to consult compilations that indicate where records are found. Otherwise, it is easy to go to, or write to, the incorrect office for a public record. Such a compilation is found in the *Handy Book for Genealogists*, edited by George B. Everton, Sr. (see the bibliography).

County records differ from local records in that they are made within the county's jurisdiction. They fall into about four categories:

1. **Court Records** such as criminal courts, civil courts, and probate courts (wills, administrations, letters of administration, etc.).

2. **Land Records** such as deeds, mortgages, and maps.

3. **Vital Records**, such as births, marriage licenses and marriage records, and death certificates.

4. **Miscellaneous Records** including naturalization records, registers of voters, and assessment and tax rolls.

Usually these are found in the county buildings at the county seat. Since they are public records, they are ordinarily available for research purposes. As in all public offices, no one is assigned to do family research, even for a fee. Information sought by mail should carry a specific request for a specific record, with the name, date, and place given and the accurate fee enclosed. It is advisable to go to the depository, but if that is impossible and a simple letter of request does not get results, the services of a record searcher should be used.

State and territorial records are usually found in the capital of the state. The Secretary of State is commonly the custodian of many early records, but he may have removed some or all of them to a State Archives building for preservation. State census records, vital records, Appellate Court papers, and state papers are among the records kept.

Possibly the largest body of public records is found at the Federal level. It should be kept in mind that Federal records do not antedate our life as a nation. Therefore, if you are searching for someone who served in the French and Indian Wars, or in King Philip's War, his name will not be found among the war service records of the United

States. The Federal period did not begin until 1776.

There is a continuing program of microfilming Federal records in order to preserve the originals while still making the records available to researchers. Among the records of most genealogical interest are the national census records, military records, service records of all United States wars, war pension applications, and death records of pensioners. There are also some shipping and passenger lists, incomplete immigration records, and passport records for 1791–1897. This is only part of the information to be found on the Federal level. As you become more skilled in research and need additional genealogical information, you will necessarily become acquainted with many more records on every level. Many of the county, state, and Federal records are so important to the beginning searcher that they will be dealt with later in this manual.

The Public Health Service, U.S. Department of Health, Education, and Welfare (HEW), has published three pamphlets that can be obtained from the Superintendent of Documents, U.S. Government Printing Office, Washington, D.C. 20402:

Where to Write for Birth and Death Records (#HMS 72–1142).

Where to Write for Marriage Records (#HMS 72–1144).

Where to Write for Divorce Records (#HMS 72–1145).

These are only three of the numerous publications that are being made available to users of the Federal records and that are designed to save a great deal of the researchers' time and effort (see the bibliography).

When you write a letter to ask for a copy of any public record, be sure to keep it simple. Government clerks do not have the time, interest, or inclination to read lengthy, rambling genealogical letters. You must be particular about what you are requesting. When you apply for a copy of a record, you should include:

1. The kind of record desired (for example, a complete death record).

2. The full name of the person whose record you want.

3. The date and place of the occurrence (the year is especially important).

4. The sex and race of the person.

A letter written succinctly, including your check for the cost of a copy of the public record, usually elicits the information you want, if it exists in the office to which you wrote. If it does not exist, the agency will return your check with an explanation. Don't always expect a full and complete record, however, for the person who originally gave the information may not have been able to answer all the questions asked. Writing such a letter is usually worth the effort, even if you receive an incomplete record (and even that may contain just what you are searching for, or a clue that will take you further).

This was well demonstrated in the case of George Anderson, who died on 12 October 1902 in Minnesota. He was known to have had a wife whom he married in 1857 in Claremont, New York, but her maiden name was unknown and she had died before he arrived in Minnesota. His own birth date and place were also unknown. Since he died in 1902, the searcher obtained a death record, which contained his death date and place of birth, but no birth date—only that he was ninety-four years old. It should have contained his parents' names and his wife's name if she had been living, but only if the person who gave the information for the death record had known these facts. This death record was taken from the records in the hospital where George died. Knowing that he had been born in Wheatland, New York, and that the date (reached by deduction) was probably around 1808, the searcher started to look in an entirely different area for his parents, as well as for a birth or baptismal record. This single death record also opened up the possibility that George Anderson had had more than one wife. (He would have been about forty-nine years old when he married—a relatively late age to take a first wife.) The search was complicated further since George had outlived all his contemporaries and anyone else who would have been able to give the searcher information. Even his only surviving son had recently died at age seventy-seven in California. Finally, however, through Federal census records, Civil War records, and deeds in New York State, Ohio, and Minnesota, the searcher managed to find the missing details of George Anderson's life.

Another example concerns Peter Forett, who arrived in a small town in New Jersey about 1850. He married there and had six children, all of whom predeceased him. In 1917, after a long and moderately successful business career, he died in the home of a grandson, who had only the vaguest information about him. The grandson knew Forett's age and place of birth, but little of what had happened to him before 1850. He remembered hearing something about his grandfather's childhood, but it was all a bit hazy in his mind. When he gave the information for the death record, he recalled that after Forett's birth, his mother had married a man named Russell Johnson (or Johnson Russell), who had been known to Forett as "Russ." Not knowing the name of Forett's father, the grandson assumed that the stepfather's name would suffice. For the purpose of making a record, it may have been sufficient in his eyes, but for anyone trying to prove Peter Forett's ancestry it was not. Other records had to be sought. As it turned out, the scribe had recorded Forett's father's name as "Johnson Russell Johnson." This was probably what the grandson stammered, or was heard to say, when it came time to give that part of the information.

In using public records, we have to recognize the fact that human beings are fallible. Not only can the person giving the information be inaccurate; so can the person recording it. For this reason it is never wise to accept a set of facts as truth until they can be checked against another record. In the case of Peter Forett this was difficult, and in the case of George Anderson it was only because an interested nurse questioned George about his family that there was any connection made with New York State.

To use the vast array of public records, the family historian should travel to the depositories at the county level, and to those in the state and national capitals, at least once. The experience of exploring records and finding evidence is one of the best parts of genealogy. Receiving letters and certificates by mail is rewarding, but the satisfaction and thrill of a visit to the public record offices—offices that have been maintained for so long by taxes we and our ancestors have paid—far surpasses the momentary thrill of opening a letter.

Many of these county, state, and Federal records are so important to the beginning searcher that they will be dealt with separately later.

6

Church Records

Church records are made purely for ecclesiastical reasons, not to provide the late twentieth-century genealogist with answers to his problems. They were, and still are, made to report to church authorities the functional success of a church in the community. These reports provide statistical proof of the weakness or strength of the church from year to year. Genealogists long ago discovered that church records, which consist basically of baptisms, memberships, marriages, and burials, form a fine primary source if they exist. Like all other records, church records have been subject to flood, fire, vermin, and loss by neglect or theft.

We tend to think of the founding of America as having been accomplished by colonists who were seeking religious liberty. We know that the profit and security motives were stronger than the desire for religious freedom, but we tend to overlook them in our idealistic approach. This leads to the assumption that church records must be available for all the places people settled, but the basic questions that must be answered before church records can be used are WHERE are the extant records located and WHEN did they begin?

During the 1930s the Works Projects Administration (WPA) planned an inventory of all United States church archives and records. The work was never finished because too many churches were unwilling to cooperate on such a project and because the amount of material discovered was too voluminous. However, as a result of this historical project many volumes were published, and these can usually be found in libraries. Naturally, the data giving the location of some of the church records is now inaccurate, especially records listed forty years ago as being in the hands of a clerk of the local church or in a minister's home. Some denominations, realizing the genealogical and historical value of keeping church records still remaining in local churches, have set up central depositories where local churches are invited to send their records for preservation and research. In general, however, in all the states the WPA volumes are still among the finest sources for locating church records. The churches of a denomination are listed together, giving name, location, brief notes concerning the history of the congregation, its dates of founding and of combining with other churches, and the location of the records as of the 1930s.

Many early church records have been copied and published either in book form or in the genealogical magazines. A number can be found in the DAR records already cited. A vast microfilming project by the Genealogical Society of the Church of Jesus Christ of Latter-day Saints has been highly successful in preserving the records of churches and making them available for research. Local copyists have been conscious of the need to preserve and make available the records of their local churches so that such copies may be found by later searchers.

There are many local churches that have not participated in these various copying projects, however. They have managed to keep their records in the church office safe, a bank vault, or the home of the pastor or a clerk. Fortunate indeed are the local church and parsonage that haven't been burned with the records in them.

One set of records in a small neighborhood church in one of our big cities was discovered lying on the floor of the pastor's study in his home. When the small church was absorbed by a larger city church, the records were sent to a board member of the larger church, who placed them on the top closet shelf in the pastor's study for safe-keeping. When they were discovered by a genealogist some thirty-five years later, they were being used as a step stool in that same closet. The pastor didn't realize how important they were, so the person who found them borrowed them with his full permission. They were copied and indexed and then returned to the top shelf of the closet. A copy of the work was given to the church so that the books would lie undisturbed until they could be deposited in a central repository where they would be microfilmed and preserved. The copyist donated a step stool to the church to ensure that meanwhile the books would remain unharmed.

In determining what churches existed at the time and place you are researching, don't give up if the church isn't listed in the *WPA Index*. Those county, state, and local histories that proliferated about the time of the country's Centennial celebration in the 1870s and 1880s usually included at least one chapter on church history. Local historians gave a surprising amount of information about the churches and in some cases were foresighted enough to include a transcript of at least part, and sometimes all, of the vital records of the leading or earliest church in their town. It is to be hoped that the day will come when no church history or local history will be published without including vital records!

Local churches will be of various moods when it comes to divulging the contents of their records. If it is necessary to write a church for a record, keep the letter very brief, stating simply your desire for a copy of a specific record, and enclose a return, self-addressed, stamped envelope and a small donation check. Even with all this careful planning you may never receive a reply. Some churches have no staff to do any searching in their unindexed volumes, which is time-consuming, and some have no one who can read the old-fashioned script in which so many church records were kept. The latter is especially true if the volumes happen to have been kept in a foreign language such as German or Swedish. The minister himself may be irked by the number of letters he receives and therefore refuse to answer any.

He can't be blamed, since, of course, he is not a clerk. There are even places where the pastor or the clerk in the church office does not know the location of the old records. I had this experience once with a church whose records are supposed to be extant from 1702. I sent several letters, but as they brought no response, I visited the church office myself. The full-time clerk in the office said that my letters had been received and that she and the pastor had been "looking for" the early records because others had sent inquiries. They knew that the old books had at one time been in a bank vault in the local bank, but the man who had put them there was deceased and the bank was sure that the books had been removed several years ago. I suggested that the books might have been sent to the denomination's own archives, an idea that had not occurred to the pastor or the clerk. A telephone call located the books in the archival library, where they had indeed been deposited about 1945. Now that particular local church has a postcard that is sent to inquirers, telling them where to write for early records.

Probably the most useful source for locating records today without a great deal of frustration and delay is E. Kay Kirkham's *A*

Survey of American Church Records, published by Everton Publishers, Inc., Logan, Utah, 1971. Mr. Kirkham has included most of the church records accumulated by the Genealogical Society in Salt Lake City, and his listing covers the major denominations before 1860, although the material is not complete for every denomination. It is a basic reference and a great time-saver, however, and covers all the states east of the Mississippi before 1860.

Once having discovered where the records you need are kept, and whether they cover the appropriate period, what can you expect from them? Remembering the purpose for which they were made, think of the denomination of the church. Was it Baptist, Roman Catholic, Methodist, Presbyterian? Since church records contain data for ecclesiastical authorities, they contain details of data important to that specific church. Some church records will show baptisms or christenings of infants; others, only baptisms of adults, marriages of members, and perhaps burials, along with officers of the church. Thus, in Baptist records few if any baptisms of infants will be found because candidates for baptism are usually fourteen years or older.

Before churches were established in new settlements, the spiritual needs of the people were very often cared for by a "preacher" who traveled from settlement to settlement. People often postponed marriages and baptisms until a preacher rode in. He would on the same day perform marriages and baptize all the children born since the last visit of a preacher. Sometimes he would even baptize the child of a couple he had just married. Not only were there no official records left behind in the churchless village, but whatever records were made by the traveling preacher rode away with him in his saddlebags. These were not official church records; they belonged to him personally, and he used them to report statistics to his authorities to prove that he was carrying on the work of his calling. This lack of church establishment, and hence the lack of records, explains what seemed to be the illegitimacy of so many first children. With no one available legally to marry a couple, the young wife was very often late into her first pregnancy when a preacher came riding by.

There are some warnings that you should heed when using church records. They are not in any way standardized; their purposes exclude that possibility. There is also the question of accuracy. Records of marriages and baptisms were not always made on the day the event took place but were entered following the event from notes the minister had made. The human factor of fallibility must, therefore, always be considered. Records for a baptism may give a month, a year, but no day. They are found with the child unnamed or simply stated to be "a child of" so and so. In marriage records the groom's full name may be stated, but only the first name of the bride, or vice versa. If the person who made the record in the church book was not familiar with the family names, they may be spelled phonetically. If an entry states that a baptized child is "of Mrs. Jones," or that the baptism of a child was performed "for Mrs. Jones," it does not necessarily mean that the father was deceased or the child illegitimate. It may simply mean that, while Mrs. Jones was a member of that church, Mr. Jones was not.

Not all vital records will be found in separately divided categories in church record books. They may be found scattered through the meeting records of the ruling body of the church: the Session Records of the Presbyterians; the Official Board records of the Methodists; the Monthly Meetings of the

Quakers, especially the Women's Monthly Meeting records.

If you find that the records have been copied instead of being microfilmed, there are further cautions. Copyists frequently worked without anyone to check the accuracy of their transcription. Sometimes early copyists omitted whole pages from their work, read names inaccurately, or even placed names in inaccurate juxtaposition, simply because they appeared that way on the original page. Unless the copyist was familiar with the names of the people who lived near the church, he would be likely to make many errors in the copy. It's better to consult a microfilm copy and transcribe what you actually see than to depend on another person's transcript.

7

Cemeteries and Their Records

One of our daughters admits that, until she was twelve years old, she didn't know that family picnics could be held anywhere but in a cemetery. Her genealogy-minded family found searching for a gravestone record a very good excuse for a drive in the country and a day in a quiet, beautiful place, with a picnic-basket lunch beneath tall trees. It was a cool, refreshing, and delightful way to spend a Saturday. It was even better if one belonged to a group of people dedicated to copying gravestone information for the use of genealogists. Groups such as these develop great camaraderie because of their basic interest in genealogy.

There are other reasons, however, for going to search in a cemetery than just to spend a nice day in the country. Gravestone information can sometimes provide missing dates and relationships. A good search can often correct misinformation received elsewhere or provide information to prove false a previously accepted statement. Clues for further searches are frequently found on a stone; and a gravestone will sometimes yield a lost bit of local color.

Many years ago we came upon a stone in an abandoned New Jersey churchyard which we had been seeking for some time. The name of the deceased and his death date were inscribed—worn, but readable. The third statement was amazing: he had died "aged 585 years." We inspected the brown Portland stone monument carefully. We finally concluded that the stonecutter had chiseled out the age as 58. When he learned that the correct age was 85, he chiseled the second 5 following the 8. Then he filled in the first 5 with a mixture of stone and mortar, leaving the correct age as 85 years. Time and weather had rubbed the mortar from the first 5, leaving the gravestone to proclaim the age at death as 585 years. After deciphering the stone, we had verification for a previously found record that the man's age had been 85 years at death, plus a colorful lost piece of local interest, the stonemaker's error. We felt that we had something to brighten the pages of the ancestor's biography.

A colonial recipe for chowder begins with the statement, "First catch a cod." A modern recipe for using a cemetery would begin, "First find the cemetery." The big, important cemeteries in large towns and cities are readily discovered through the telephone book, but not all our forebears lived in cities. In addition to big city cemeteries, there are churchyards where customarily only members of the church are buried. There are government cemeteries for soldiers and important politicians. There are privately owned cemeteries where lots can be purchased for a fee from a corporation that cares for the graves. There are family cemeteries that were set up on a man's farm when transportation was difficult, and that are now abandoned and forgotten—overgrown with trees and weeds.

These latter cemeteries, and the old churchyards where the church no longer exists, can frequently be the most rewarding to the searcher, if he can find them. Drastic changes in the uses of land have caused many private family burying grounds to disappear. The burial record handed down in a Mott family of Long Island states that a son of a Revolutionary War soldier is buried beside a Selden road on the Island, "next to a telegraph pole," with the number of the pole given in the record. It is suspected that the soldier was also buried on that piece of property next to his son, who had cared for him in his old age, but no stone marks either interment. Eventually a road was cut through, poles were erected, and the little family burying place was destroyed. Only the numbered telegraph pole, if it still remains, reveals their last resting place, now forgotten in the ongoing march of time and people.

Very often the growth of towns and villages wiped out whole burial areas before the states passed laws to protect them. One such instance is the old First Presbyterian Church Cemetery in Newark, New Jersey, where interments went back to the days of the founding of the village of Newark. Now the cemetery property is covered with blacktop and is a vast parking area. Some of the gravestones were gathered and buried in a single crypt in another burying ground and a record was made of them. The relationships are now difficult to prove even through other existing records, for the early records of the church were destroyed when the British burned Newark during the Revolution.

Not every grave has a stone marker as a memorial. Many people have been buried with nothing to mark the place and with no public or private record made of the time of their passing. If the person was buried in a cemetery with no headstone marking the grave, we can only hope that there were some records available to identify him.

Burial records have suffered the same fate as other records and are often nonexistent for the eighteenth and early nineteenth centuries. They will be found in as many places as there are kinds of cemeteries. Some are in a cemetery office, either public or private. Some are in the records of churches. Some will be found in collections made and deposited in libraries of genealogical or historical societies. There are many places to look if a gravestone is not found—and this will be frequently, considering the number of stones that have been destroyed by vandals or have crumbled through the years.

The interments found in church records were made either by the minister who read the burial service or by the sexton who had charge of the burial site in the churchyard. Ministers often kept their own private burial records, and these may sometimes tell more than the church records. Sextons kept records of the graves they dug and who was buried in them; these are often useful to supplement or replace the lost records of church or minister. Churchyard records contain the name and the popularly known age of the deceased, and sometimes his relationship to others in the community or others in the same burial site. There may even be a record of a nonmember husband or wife, buried beside his or her spouse who was a church member. If the grave is marked in the churchyard, it is well to also examine nearby stones and to add the data to your notes on others of the same name. Families tend to bury all members close to each other. This was done originally in expectation of the Resurrection Day when they hoped that they would arise together as a spiritual body. Stones for unknown children, unmarried cousins, aunts or uncles, slaves or faithful servants, can often verify or add names that you had not found elsewhere in your records.

If you cannot find a gravestone or a record of burial in a churchyard, it is wise to suspect a cemetery set up on the family farm. You may find it deserted and overgrown on the edge of a road or deep in woods that have reclaimed the land. Some of these private cemeteries have stones that have been copied through the efforts of local groups, possibly by DAR members, but it is safe to say that there are thousands across the country that are still undiscovered and unrecorded. These stones may hold the answers to untold thousands of genealogical questions. If each of us could copy the stones in just one such cemetery a year, either near our home or wherever we vacation, and then deposit our copies in a library or historical society, imagine what a far-reaching effect such volunteer work would have!

Genealogists of earlier generations copied the inscriptions on the stones in many graveyards. In the years that have elapsed, some of those cemeteries have disappeared or, if they are still in existence, some of their stones have disappeared or have become illegible. These earlier copies of inscriptions can be found in numerous local societies or in church offices.

Town cemeteries are usually run much like a private enterprise, with a governing board, an office, and caretakers. Sometimes there is a main office in charge of a superintendent whose duties include overseeing the property, making funeral arrangements, and keeping track of who is buried where.

Legal rules and regulations now control some of these cemeteries so that records are available. Not all of them have records before 1890. Some do, but they may not be complete. Generally, by 1890 a cemetery corporation was recording the death data as it appeared on the death certificate presented by the undertaker. Family relationships and lines of descent on file with these offices are usually very helpful, for they can tell a great deal about the deceased and his family.

As an aside, if you are presuming that you will be buried in a family plot in a town cemetery because you think you are entitled to be as a descendant of the original owner, and if there are any remaining full or partially full graves, it is suggested that you check with the office of that cemetery and have the matter of the current ownership of the plot cleared so that you will have your name on record as a deserving descendant for burial. This kind of foresighted care can avoid great distress for your family when you die, for they are probably ignorant of the current burial regulations in the "family plot" in your state.

Besides town cemeteries there are cemeteries owned by private corporations, which are sometimes called Memorial Parks. Here, as in town cemeteries, there is usually a set of burial records. These are not considered public records, and it is often necessary to pay a fee for the information sought. There is one cemetery corporation in a western Pennsylvania town of some size through which emigrants passed in great numbers on their way to Ohio and the West. A searcher sent three letters asking for a complete copy of any record they had on a certain Revolutionary War soldier, since family records showed that he was buried there. There was no reply to any of the letters. Finally the searcher was authorized to go to the town, which is a county seat. He found the cemetery gates chained and locked, with no one in attendance. The County Clerk's office said that indeed there were several volumes of burial records of that cemetery, but they were kept by a local gentleman in the vault of the local bank, of which he was the president. The searcher made an effort to see the bank president, but since he had seen the name of the searcher on the three letters written, he "was not available." It was learned from the gentleman's secretary that he considered the cemetery records confidential; that he felt no one had any right to know what they contained; that a person's age and cause of death were no one's affair; that the dead were buried and should be allowed to lie in peace. When the secretary was asked who made the entries in the records when someone was buried in that cemetery, she replied that the bank president did—that he went to the vault twice a year and made all the entries for the preceding six months at the same time. One could consider this an extreme case, but it makes a point about accuracy, for who knows how accurate records are, even if they are obtainable?

The searcher in this case did not give up. The next day he decided to walk around the periphery of the cemetery, following the iron fence that enclosed it and hoping that the stone he was seeking would be near the fence so he could read or take a picture of it. As he walked, he came to a road that seemed to divide the cemetery into two separate sections. What appeared to be an older section lay across the road and up a hill, and was unfenced. Near the top of the hill, in what was evidently a family plot, was the stone of the Revolutionary War soldier. Not only his name but his wife's name and several of his children's names were recorded on the shaft.

Not all cemeteries and their records are as strictly controlled as this one. Their records may not extend too far into the past, but the cooperation of the office is usually available, although often dilatory. In New York State, as in other places where there is a body of regulations concerning cemeteries, a complaint to the State Cemetery Agency will usually assure prompt attention to requests. There is no national standard set for the contents of cemetery records, but what are usually found are name, age or birth date, date of interment, marital status, cause of death, location of the grave, and either the name of the attending physician or the undertaker. This is a copy of the death certificate as presented by the undertaker when he makes arrangements for burial. It is compiled from the answers given to the undertaker's questions by a survivor, who may or may not have had accurate information. This is true of all death records; and when we consider gravestone inscriptions, it becomes evident from some of them that the informant was not accurate.

A point that must be carefully considered is: Who gave the information that appears on the death certificate or cemetery record or gravestone? In some cities modern death records contain the name of the informant, but it is not a universal practice. Generally the postdecease information is given by a person who should know the facts, but it can also be given by someone who makes an educated guess, thinking that such data are not important, or who didn't know the deceased intimately. Perhaps the deceased has survived both his contemporaries and his children. Even if relatives remain, grief can play havoc with memories. Birth data can be distorted through the years as men and women try to hide their true age.

In one case the age of a beloved father was unknown, since he had been orphaned early in his childhood and put out as a parish charge when he was old enough to work on a farm. No one ever considered his birthdays as he grew up. When he married the girl on the next farm, he decided to figure out his age. He chose 1868 as the year of his birth since that was the birth year of his wife; they had known each other for so long that it seemed they had been born the same year. When he died, 1868 was put on his gravestone as his year of birth. It was not until the family genealogy was in preparation that his name was found on the 1860 census. He had been a two-year-old in the household of parents who died very shortly afterward. Thus, he was born in 1858 and was ten years older than his wife. In this case the family was not at fault when they gave 1868 as his birth year, but it does show that we must be skeptical of any date on records—death records, cemetery records, and gravestones— until we have considered them in the light of what other records reveal.

Geography plays an important part in finding cemetery records. In the very earliest days of the colonies we know that the dead were buried on their own farms or near the spot where they died and that frequently no records can be found and only an approximate date can be calculated from other data. For instance, the death date may have to be inferred from a will or administration. Land for burials was often provided by deed as a gift or set aside by the town fathers, but no provision was made to keep records of the persons buried there. Town lines changed with the expansion and proliferation of settlements. A man may have owned land and lived on it all his life, yet his land may have been within the boundaries of different towns or villages at different periods. To find his place of burial, a search must be made not only in one town but in a whole area.

Genealogical and historical societies, state libraries, and archives very often have extensive collections of gravestone and cemetery records. Copying gravestones has been a hobby or a cause for many individuals and groups for decades. The DAR, in its search for Revolutionary War ancestors, has had hundreds of volumes of cemetery records and inscriptions collected by its members all across the country. Copies are supposed to be deposited in the state library and in the DAR library in Washington, D.C. In some historical societies the cemetery and gravestone records are found supplemented by card files of data taken from church records or local newspapers. These are especially helpful, since they bring together three sources: cemetery records, church records, and newspaper obituaries.

Individuals who copy gravestones and monuments have treated their collected materials in many ways. Some deposited the original handwritten loose sheets or notebooks, unindexed, with the local historical or genealogical society. Some have published, either as separate books or in genealogical magazines;

and again, like church records, they may be found in magazines out of the original area. Only in rare instances do we find that these copying efforts have been checked by another person. Don't forget—it is almost inevitable that errors are present, unwittingly created by the copyist.

Careful checking is highly desirable with any copied record, but it cannot provide corrections for original errors made by survivors of the deceased. An accurate death date and other details of demise must therefore be sought by considering peripheral data as well. This is a cardinal principle in all genealogical research: be skeptical of everything until one fact is checked against another.

8

Deeds and Mortgages

If a will can be considered a man's memorial, deeds can be considered the solid base on which the memorial rests. Deeds definitely locate a man geographically and place him on one or more pieces of terra firma at some time during his lifetime. It has been truly said that if a man ever owned even a tiny piece of land, he can be traced through the land records. Men who were not farmers had to have some place to live, and our history shows that one of their first American dreams was to own their own homes.

A deed or conveyance is a civil contract prescribed by law between two parties, one of whom contracts to convey a specified property to which he holds legal title to a second party, named, who provides a specific consideration, usually money, of equal value. The purpose of a deed is to establish the facts of legal ownership, leaving no doubt as to the extent of that ownership.

Since deeds are legal instruments or civil contracts, they must contain certain necessary parts. Their phraseology, unfortunately for many researchers, is the outgrowth of generations of Latin verbiage. This is slowly changing now, and documents of all kinds are being criticized for their "gobbledygook" language. But no matter how soon or how extensive those changes are, the researcher will still have to cope with the older forms when doing research in earlier periods. Whether modern or not, deeds contain set phrases that are legally accurate in that they are acceptable and presumed to be incontestable. The parts of deeds required to make them legal and acceptable for registering are of most interest to the genealogist. They are the portions that he will abstract whether he obtains a photocopy, or does the work in the courthouse from the books in which the deeds are recorded, or uses microfilm copies:

1. Name(s) of conveyor(s) or seller(s), also known as grantor(s), and place(s) of residence; perhaps occupation(s).

2. The consideration (usually an amount of money) given by the grantee, and acknowledgment of its receipt by the grantor.

3. Name(s) and place(s) of residence of grantee(s) (buyers).

4. An accurate description of the property being conveyed.

5. The seller's guarantee that the purchaser will not have any interference in his enjoyment of the property and his guarantee that he is the legal owner and may legally sell it.

6. The requisite number of witnesses to the deed as prescribed by the state.

7. The date of the deed or conveyance.

The necessary legal parts can be seen in this abbreviated deed:

1. I, Benjamin Birdsell of Rye in the County of Westchester Province of New York yeoman for and

2. in consideration of £19 current lawful money of the Province of New York to me in hand paid before the sealing and delivery of these presents by John Clapp

3. of the Township of Greenwich in Fairfield County Colony of Connecticut the receipt of which I do hereby acknowledge and

4. do confirm unto him the said John Clapp his heirs and assigns all that certain

tract of land lying in the Township of Rye in the County of Westchester and Province of New York containing 7 acres and nine tenths acres butted and bounded as follows viz east by Blind Brook south by Antony Fields land north by said John Clapp land and running westerly from said Blind Brook until it makes the above quantity of acres

5. To Have and to hold the said granted and bargained tract of land with all appurtenances and commodities to same . . . unto him the said John Clapp his heirs and assigns to their one and only proper use and benefit forever and I do covenant promise and grant that before the insealing and delivery hereof I am the true sole and lawful owner of the above bargained premises and possessed of the same in my own right as a good and absolute estate of inheritance in fee simple

Signed   beniamin birdsell

6. 10 April 1742

7. Witnessed by   Moses Prall
Jeremiah Erskine
John Mehiel

As paper became more readily obtainable, after the colonial period, more and more people began to use printed legal forms.

These printed deeds continued to have all the necessary legal parts, but did relieve the clerks and scribes of nearly half their former labor. Today the lawyer's typist cuts that labor still further while continuing to maintain legalities. This quitclaim deed of 1910 illustrates:

"Form 2018—Quit Claim Deed"
"Matthias Plum, Law Blank Publisher"

THIS INDENTURE

Made the *twenty-Eighth* day of *March*
in the year of our Lord
One Thousand Nine Hundred and *ten*
BETWEEN *David T R Stryker*
of the *township* of *Chester* in the County
of *Morris* and State of *New Jersey*
of the First Part;
AND *David Stryker*
of the *township* of *Chester* in the County
of *Morris* and State of *New Jersey*
of the Second Part
WITNESSETH That the said party
of the first part in consideration
of the sum of *one dollar*
To him duly paid before the delivery hereof
has remised released and forever quit claimed

to the said party of the second part ALL *that certain tract or parcel of land* . . .

The italic words are those which were filled in on the printed blank. The description of the land being conveyed was filled in in longhand, for even as late as 1910 typewriters were not found in many lawyer's offices. All the necessary legalities are contained in this printed form, but it can be seen from the excerpt given here what a laborsaving device it became. It also made the work of reading easier for the researcher.

Before the days of typewriters, carbon paper, and mechanical duplicators, deeds were entirely handwritten. At least two identical copies were made by the scribe on a large piece of parchment or paper. The grantor and the grantee each received one of the duplicate copies, which were separated by cutting them apart in a wavy or scalloped pattern. This gave assurance that, in any future necessary comparison of the deeds, they would be identified by the shape and fit of the cuts. This wavy or scalloped indenting of each of the documents gave rise to the name "indenture" for a document.

As with wills, there is a variety of deeds or indentures. Although they differ in many ways, all of them are legally binding agreements between two parties to enter into reciprocal arrangements. A gift or gratuitous deed is one made without cash payment. An example is when a father deeds land to a married son or daughter in lieu of devising property to him or her in his will, or in gratitude for the care a son or daughter "has so lovingly given" him. (These same sentiments and phrases are also found in wills in which parents provide for division of their land among their heirs.)

If a son married and moved to another area with his young family, or if he had already acquired sufficient land through his own efforts, sometimes his siblings inherited his share of land at the father's death. In this case a claim could be drawn up to relieve the recipient of the inheritance to which he was originally entitled. These claims were called quitclaims or partition deeds. Usually a brother or a sister became the recipient and everyone was happy. These partition or quitclaims clearly defined who owned what specific part of an inheritance and very often clarified misunderstandings concerning the extent of inherited land.

Quitclaim deeds are also made by heirs so that land involved in an intestate estate settlement can be sold. In these, the names and addresses of children can often be found, some of them represented by attorney because of the distance they live from the estate. Many of these deeds reveal the married names and addresses of daughters.

Even when the grantee (purchaser) doesn't sign the deed, he is bound by its covenant. He cannot, for instance, claim more land than the deed specifies he has paid for. A deed is binding on the grantor (seller) only from the moment of its delivery to the purchaser, which usually does not occur until the deed is examined for its legality and registered in the proper public office.

To the genealogist the information in deeds can be of the greatest value. Not only do they definitely locate a man geographically, sometimes even naming his wife, but frequently they give his occupation and place him at a specific time:

This indenture made the 14th day of June Anno Domini 1704 between John Barber of the town of East Hampton in the County of Suffolk upon the Island of Nassau in the Colony of New-York in America mason of the oneth part and Mathias Burnet of the same place cordwainer of the other part.

Note that in the example no punctuation appears. Punctuation is not regarded in deeds, and often the rapid flow of phrases will be confusing. Careful reading however, will allow the sense and intent to come through, and the beginner will be able to abstract the needed information.

Sometimes a deed will give a clue to the parents of the grantor: "the land *my father Moses* purchased of Joseph Smidt"; or, "the homelot left me by *my father John deceased*"; or ". . . land next to the Three Acre Lott *my father Reuben* received from *my grandfather Israel*." Discovering phrases such as these is like picking up golden coins in a barren field. They can make the day.

The economic status of the family may also be determined in a deed by the size of the lands bought or sold. Immigrants have always been land hungry in America, but some have been able to put together quite large estates that then benefited succeeding generations.

The first deed found in any particular area may show the previous place of residence for a family, and the last deed registered may show that they moved elsewhere. These are especially helpful when one is searching for a family on the move, or heading westward. The last deed could also coincide with the retirement of an older person and his moving in with a son or daughter, a more common practice in the eighteenth than in the twentieth century. If this is suspected, it is well to check other records before deciding that the older person died about the time his land was sold.

Deeds that transfer land to members of the same family can show relationships or reveal the names of married daughters: "To Sarah Marlowe my daughter widow of Henry Marlowe of the second part . . . for the tenderness and love she bears to me" . . . signed Eleazer Miller.

The names of neighbors on adjacent properties can often help solve the question of whom the children married, since, as pointed out earlier, young men who worked hard all day were not inclined to go too far when they courted and often found a wife on the next farm or in the same urban neighborhood. Propinquity has always played a large part in romance, even in the cities, so it is well to know who lived north, east, south, and west of the home place.

Like wills, deeds are public records and will usually be found indexed in books in the County or Town Clerk's offices. As these old volumes become more and more frayed with use, they are being microfilmed and retired. The Index volumes are usually labeled "Grantor" and "Grantee," or "Direct" and "Indirect." Some offices are becoming more modern and labeling them "Buyers" and "Sellers," but whatever label they bear, the Index is the first place to look for the names you are seeking. In the Index you will find name, date, and reference to volume and page where the full deed has been recorded. Modern recordings are typed rather than handwritten as they were formerly, making the work of reading much easier. There may also be reference to recordings of mortgages, liens, or sheriff's sales. Make certain that you see all the references listed. If you can't find what you are looking for, ask for help, but be sure to take your references accurately before doing so.

Mortgages can be almost as revealing as deeds, for personal as well as real property may be mortgaged. Mortgages on the stocks of store shelves, on farm animals, on crops in the field, or on cargoes of ships can be found. The owner of the things mortgaged (the mort-mortgagor) does not part with the properties he has borrowed against. He continues to live on the land or in the town house, or to sell the stocks on the shelves of his store, but the title does not belong to him until he pays off the full amount he borrowed. He may rent to someone else in the meantime, but he is still liable for the mortgage money, which is, after all, borrowed money.

In law, when the full amount of the mortgage plus interest is not repaid, the mortgage is then treated like a true deed or conveyance. If the owner subsequently sells, it is considered a lien against the property, which must be paid before a new deed for the sale may be drawn, in order to clear the lien.

Mortgages are recorded in either town or county offices in the area where the mortgagor lives; if he is a nonresident, in the area of the property. The property must be described accurately, as is true in a deed. It is sometimes possible to recon-struct a man's financial life by tracing how he used his properties—for instance, how he mortgaged and repaid, sometimes purchasing other desirable property with the borrowed money. All this kind of information is valuable for inclusion in your final preparation of the family history. Ideally, it will reconstruct all phases of the ancestor's life.

RECORD OF DEED ABSTRACT

DEED of _____

(Grantor _____ or Grantee _____)

Location _____

(Town, County, State; Court House or other) (Date found)

Book _____ Page _____

Grantor(s) _____ Residence _____

_____   _____

Status _____

Grantee(s) _____ Residence _____

_____   _____

Status _____

Date signed _____ Acknowledged _____ Recorded _____

Consideration _____

Description of property _____

_____

_____

_____

_____

_____

_____

_____

_____

Witnesses _____

Signed with full name _____ By mark _____

Have copy of original _____

Have photocopy of recording _____

Notes: _____

_____

9

Probate Records

On this 25th day of October, eighteen forty-two I, John Martin, of Washington County, State of New York, iron worker, being of sound mind but frail of body, do make this my last will and testament . . . . To my beloved wife Mary Martin I give all my personal and real estate . . . . My wife Mary to bring up my son Henry Martin in the fear of God . . . and to educate him into the ministry as he desires . . . all expenses to be paid from the proceeds of sale of my properties as deemed necessary . . . . I appoint my wife Mary, my brother Henry Martin, my brother-in-law Henry Wilkes executors. Witnesses Ellen Wilkes and Peter Jones. Signed John Martin.

This is a simple will that answers the basic genealogical questions of WHO: John

Martin; WHEN: 25 October 1842; and WHERE: Washington County, New York. It places the deceased in the center of his personal environment. He was an iron-worker; he had been thrifty and had acquired some properties by the time he died. He apparently had but one son and no daughters, since only one son is named in the will. His brother Henry Martin and his brother-in-law Henry Wilkes are made executors. Therefore, we can assume that John's wife had been Mary Wilkes before her marriage and that interfamily relationships were friendly. Ellen Wilkes, one of the witnesses, is not to be overlooked as also a probable relative. Then there is that last, perfect, personal touch added to the will—the signature that shows John Martin's descendants how their ancestor wrote his own name. In this case, it was a man more skillful with the tools of his trade than with a pen, but he did not sign with a mark, thus exhibiting some degree of education. As a memorial of the one who makes a will, there is nothing much better from which the family historian can learn about the ancestor.

Wills are found in many places. Genealogical collections in libraries frequently contain published or typed abstracts or indexes of wills and administrations. These can be helpful; however, it is always advisable to examine either the original will itself if it is on file, or an official copy of it in the court of probate. (This is a court where a judge determines if a will is valid.)

States have different names for their courts of probate: Circuit, County, District, Orphan's, Probate, Superior, or Surrogate. Usually, but not always, probate records will be found in a court that has a county boundary. In Rhode Island, however, the records are kept by towns and the state is divided into Probate Districts. It will be necessary to determine which court holds the will you want. (The simplest way is to ask the Town or County Clerk.) Learning this kind of thing about a place before you go there and keeping a record of that information can obviously save you a great deal of trouble.

There are genealogical sources in the court of probate other than wills. Usually good indexes are kept of all probated wills and the accompanying papers filed with them, so the first place to look is in the available indexes. The variety of papers on file will include administrations, administration bonds, inventories of estates, accounts filed by estate executors, court decrees of distribution, final settlements, legal guardianship for minors, assignment of dower, and some prenuptial agreements. Not every will that is probated is accompanied by all these papers; but certainly if there is no will for the deceased, there may be an administration of his estate that would have produced quite a file. If you can't find what you want through the indexes provided in the clerk's office, ask for help. These are public records you want to consult.

A will is a legal instrument made by a competent person called the testator. There are numerous kinds of wills that fulfill different purposes.

A **Joint Will** is one made by a husband and wife, or two siblings. These are no longer common, but they do exist:

> Christopher Hoogland and Catharine Cregier, joined in marriage . . . the testator being sickly and the testatrix . . . sound of body . . . they the testators out of special love and natural affection in matrimony received, declare that the whole estate shall go to the survivor for life. If the survivor remarry, an equal division is to be made between the children . . . the survivor shall not be obliged to give any

account of the estate to the orphan masters of this city or to the testator's friends. (New York Will Abstracts: 1:142)

A **Holographic Will** is one written, dated, and signed in the testator's own handwriting. If it was properly witnessed and its provisions were legal, there was usually no difficulty in proving such a will valid and it should be on record. Such a will is acceptable for probate only if it meets all the legal requirements.

A **Nuncupative Will** is one that is spoken or dictated to dispose of personal property in case of sudden illness or imminent death. A witness is necessary to prove the validity of this kind of will. It has to be reduced to writing and presented to a probate court, usually within two weeks, unless there are extenuating circumstances. These wills are sometimes called "battlefield wills," because of the mortally wounded soldier whose only alternative was to explain to his buddy or hospital attendants what to do with his personal belongings. In case of a serious civilian accident, when the victim knows that he cannot survive, or when someone falls unexpectedly into the terminal stages of an incurable disease, a nuncupative will can be important:

Know all persons whom it may concern that we whose names are hereunto subscribed, being called to the house of Isaac Mulford as evidences, were present and heard him make this verbal or nuncupative will in words to the following effect: "I give to my grandson Isaac Mulford Huntting my hay and my wearing clothes and also my great Bible, and all the rest of my personal estate I give to my two granddaughters namely Abigail Conklin and Mehitable Jones after my debts are paid to be equally divided." The above nuncupative will was made November the 18th day, anno domini 1772 in the presence of us, Linus Dibble, Ruth Huntting, Phebe Huntting.

Isaac Mulford signed, and the signature is very obviously that of either a very ill or a very old man.

When there is a rift in the family, a person may make an **Unofficious Will**. In this will the testator disregards the natural obligations of inheritance and leaves his property to strangers or organizations. We may read about this kind of will in the newspapers, since families and relatives frequently institute proceedings to break such a will. Sometimes a wealthy person devises large sums for establishment of a home for stray cats or dogs, or leaves a whole fortune to be used exclusively for the care, feeding, and comfort of a beloved animal. It is also considered an unofficious will when the testator, disregarding all his blood relatives, signs his whole estate to some person who has taken care of him or has been a companion. The proceedings of the court when such a will is contested and the final administration of the estate will form part of the record.

Today, the best way to study a will and its contents, or any estate papers in connection with it, is to get a photocopy of the material. There are many public offices, however, where this is still not possible. It then becomes necessary to do a transcript, abstract, or excerpt (as described in Chapter 2) or have one done by a reliable record searcher. The clerks in the probate office must not be expected to do the research, for they have all they can handle in their daily routines. If you find through correspondence that a will is extant and then send a succinct letter and check to cover the fee, you can sometimes obtain a photocopy, which you will have plenty of time to study carefully.

By the time you have reached the point of consulting public records, you should have formed the well-developed habit of noting the date, the place where the document was found, and the book (or liber) and page on which it occurred in the original record. There is nothing so frustrating as to make a real "find" and not remember where you found it.

If you must transcribe a will yourself by hand because no copying machine is available, don't forget to note any unusual spellings, sentence constructions, or word uses. (Underline them or mark them "sic"—just so.) They add to the interest when you put together the family history. Modern wills do not ordinarily have peculiarities of this kind, but probably a century from now some of the acceptable phrases of today will seem as outmoded as some we find in nineteenth-century documents. Obviously, a person devoted to Women's Liberation would hardly relish the idea of calling a wife "chattel" or "relict" as women were so often legally described in public documents. It is even difficult to believe that there were so many "dearly beloved" husbands or wives, as they were often referred to in wills.

When you receive a photocopy of an original or recorded will that was handwritten, it is well to make a typed copy of it. Do it carefully, however, and be sure not to omit phrases. Copy each word exactly; spell the names just as they appear, even if you disagree with the spelling. You will need a typed copy for inclusion in your final family history.

Some people prefer to keep information about a will and from a will on a form that can be slipped into their permanent notebook. Printed forms for this purpose can be purchased, but it is easy enough to prepare forms suitable to your own uses (see following page). There are certain facts that should be noted in abbreviated form from a specific will in addition to where and when it was found. Included should be: the name of the testator; his residence; the status and state of health if he gave it; any special provisions made for handling the estate; the bequests—to whom, along with any restrictions; the signature of the testator (written or by mark); the date the will was signed and the names of executors and witnesses; the date proved; and any other documents named that were found associated with the estate. Whether you use a form to collect these data or whether you just take notes, these are the

RECORD OF WILL ABSTRACT

WILL of _____

Location (Town, County, State) _____

Date seen (Original or recording) _____

Will Book _____ Folio _____ Date signed _____ Date proved _____

Residence of decedent _____

Status and state of health if given _____

Special provisions _____

_____

Bequests, with restrictions if any _____

_____

_____

_____

_____

_____

_____

_____

_____

Witnesses _____

Decedent signed by mark _____ by signature _____

Proved by: _____

Executor(s) _____

Other documents associated with this estate _____

_____

Have copy of original _____

Have photocopy of recording _____

Notes: _____

_____

_____

_____

_____

124

specific details from the will that should be included so that you have a full record of the intent of the testator.

A person who has died without a will is said to have died intestate. If there is an estate, real or personal, an administrator is assigned by the court. He then becomes accountable to the court for his actions in connection with disposing of the estate. It is in such cases that the dockets of papers can become very useful in determining who the members of the family are and what their status is at the time of the division of the property. Very careful examination of these papers is advised, for even so much as an overlooked sentence may contain a very valuable clue. For example, when a man with children dies without a will, under the law both his sons and daughters should share equally the proceeds of his estate. If a daughter (or son) predeceases a parent, her (or his) children are entitled to the portion that daughter or son would have received and are therefore often named in the will. In this way a will sometimes reveals the names of a deceased man's grandchildren. It can also verify that a child has predeceased him. In the case of married daughters, their married names and often the names of their husbands can be discovered. If the settlement papers are not available in an intestate estate, sometimes the deeds showing sale of property by descendants will give this same kind of information, and members of the family can be traced through these deeds.

When minor children have been left by a parent who has died intestate, their interests in that estate are protected by law. The term "minor" or "infant" used in many of the resulting records does not mean that the orphan was a small babe in arms. It means that the young person was not of legal age and lacked one or both parents, so that the courts had to act to protect him and his rightful inheritance. In this kind of situation, Orphan's Court records can be another valuable source of information. Very often an orphan, if he was over fifteen years old, could choose a close relative as guardian. If he was under fourteen or fifteen, the court assigned a competent guardian to act in his behalf. In some cases the guardian took full charge of him, taking him into his own home, but it was just as likely that the orphan would be left with his surviving parent and his legal guardian would oversee his legal interests.

When no will and no administration of an intestate estate are found, it will be necessary to use other sources to establish the names of the family members. Don't be discouraged by the lack of wills and administrations—not everyone who came to America achieved success or accumulated enough wealth to leave a will as his memorial. If one of your own ancestors left no will, it may be that *you* are his memorial.

10

Military Records

Your great-great-grandfather was Major Hiram Jones, or a Colonel, or some other officer who served in a war. Like all other broad family statements, this family tradition must either be proved or disproved. Questioning people in the family who have also heard the tradition may help to pinpoint in what war the man served and where he was living at the time. With only this meager information you can begin to search for proof of service in extant military records. Don't be disappointed if you discover that your great-great-grandfather Jones was a private. Traditions have a tendency to exaggeration.

Your search for proof on a colonial soldier may take you from local to state to national depositories before you find and can document the true status and service of your Hiram Jones, because, unfortunately, there is no central depository for colonial military records. On the contrary, they are found scattered among the thirteen original states in their state archives, town records, historical societies, or even private hands. Patriotic societies and large libraries often have some of the finest colonial military records in their manuscript collections. For some states there are published colonial military records, along with Revolutionary War and Civil War service records, but there is no general standardization. You will have to learn for yourself where the records of colonial wars that you need are maintained, if they exist at all.

During our colonial period when men were called upon to fight to defend their settlements, they automatically became eligible for service at age sixteen. As early as 1637 when the settlers in the Connecticut River Valley achieved a twenty-year period of peace by nearly annihilating the Pequot Indians, wars were fought that called for prepared fighters. The local eligibles joined the small local militia, which elected its own officers and met for drills at regular intervals. They were called members of the "train band" in the records because their weekly drills were their training periods. If records still exist of the men who were members of train bands, they are usually found in town records or printed in local histories. There is no central depository for them, but some state archives or large historical societies may have collected them.

When England fought her colonial wars on the American continent, she sent her own soldiers and mercenaries from other countries here to do the fighting. She demanded that local colonial troops and supplies be raised to supplement the men from abroad. Local volunteers and local militia responded for campaigns in the French and Indian Wars (1753–63) and Pontiac's uprising of 1763–64. Records of these militiamen will not be found in the National Archives, but many of them will be found printed in local histories or collected in historical and genealogical societies. The exploits of the ill-equipped and poorly fed men who answered England's many calls and demands have added largely to local traditions and local histories. The men who survived the campaigns told of their hardships, victories, and defeats, accounts that can be found in diaries of the period and recorded in town records. Many of their stories have been expanded into short stories and novels that re-create the atmosphere of the period. Fictionalization based on historic facts in this manner can add to the genealogist's knowledge and help re-create the early times in which a family lived.

There are, for instance, family traditions of colonials who themselves protected their homes and properties, and of others who lived near a fort for the protection afforded. These will not be found in military records, but they do add a great deal to the family history if they are admittedly family traditions. If documentation can be found to substantiate the facts, the traditions become invaluable. The story of the death of one Edward Bobet is in this latter category. It is told by William Bradford Browne in his *Babbitt Family History:*

We must depend upon tradition for the account of Edward Bobet's last hours. This tradition has been so faithfully handed down from generation to generation and seems so fully confirmed by his place of burial that there is no reason to disbelieve it. According to this tradition Bobet returned to his house to secure some necessary article—perhaps the cheese hoop, as the story says: he was accompanied by his dog in the thought that perhaps warning of prowling savages would be given by it.

He secured the needed article and was on his way back to the fort at Taunton when he became aware of his pursuit by Indians; he climbed a tree and was effectually hidden, but his faithful dog disclosed his presence and his life was the forfeit of his hazardous adventure. His grave is in a private yard, near Berkley Bridge, and is thought to be the spot where he was killed. The spot was marked by a bronze Memorial Tablet in 1911—its cost being defrayed by small contributions from his descendants from all over the United States and Canada.

When he failed to return to the fort the searching party probably buried his mutilated body where it was found and later the old headstone was placed there, which is now in Historical Hall, it having been taken away from the grave in after years and placed on a stone wall near by. This old stone reads: "Edward Bobbett Kld June 1675."

The War for Independence marked the beginning of official United States military records, but until the founding of our National Archives in Washington, D.C., in 1934 these records were not available at a central depository. The Adjutant General's office collected the service records of the Revolutionary War soldiers from local muster rolls and payrolls, which may or may not have been complete. At the National Archives each soldier's record was listed on a card showing his name, rank, military unit and colony, and the dates when his name appeared on one or more rolls. There is no genealogical information in these simple records, but they are important to the searcher who wants to establish that a soldier, sailor, or marine served in the Revolution.

The National Archives also has some other Revolutionary War records which have been indexed on cards by the soldiers' names. Don't overlook these in your search for service records, for they are varied, including data from diaries, correspondence, enlistment papers, receipts, rosters, oaths of allegiance, etc.[*]

After the establishment of the United States, the country was involved in disagreements, skirmishes, and wars that produced military involvement and military records. Many books have been published contain-

[*]See Colket and Bridgers, *Guide to Genealogical Records in the National Archives.*

ing rosters and even biographies of men who served. These can be found in libraries and historical societies where local histories are kept. They often contain anecdotes that have been lost in family traditions, some giving the local color and flavor to that part of the family history.

When I was a child, my maternal grandmother consigned to the furnace a large woolen overcoat because it was so moth- and mouse-eaten that it was almost in shreds. There was a separate piece of fabric that accompanied the coat into the flames, and it, too, was in the same sad condition. Grandmother told me that the coat had been made for her grandfather by his mother from wool from sheep on their own farm. The coat went with him when he joined the local colonial rebels. He was wearing it, as this was the easiest way to carry it, when a group of British soldiers chased him and his companions through the woods in Greenwich Village in Manhattan. He was among the last to vault a stone wall, his coattail flying out behind him. In an attempt to kill him, a British redcoat with drawn sword in hand grabbed the coattail and severed it, just as shots from the fleeing rebels already in the woods felled many of the pursuing British.

Grandma's grandfather reached over the wall and retrieved his coattail, which returned home with him and his greatcoat. Many years later, after I had given up hope of ever documenting this minor incident, I came upon Lossing's *Pictorial Field Book of the Revolution*. In the story of the retreat of Washington's army from Manhattan, this story of the coattail, which had been dismissed as unprovable family tradition, was recorded in all the details my grandmother passed on to me. A further confirmation of the importance of greatcoats to their owners came through a simple entry found in a diary of 1790, "he wore his great coat until May 31st every year, no matter what the weather" (Baxter's *Journal*, 1790–1833).

Military service records, like all other records, were made for a specific purpose. Among the early service rosters may sometimes be found a "size list." This was a list that named a soldier and described him physically, giving color of hair and eyes, height, and in some instances his civilian occupation. These lists were useful in identifying a wounded or deceased soldier after an engagement or battle. They were also a source of the occupations of specialists who might be needed in service. If a soldier was listed as a house carpenter, he could be assigned to build temporary movable barracks or to superintend the moving of permanent quarters when a new site was needed. Shipbuilders, shoemakers, carpenters—the craftsmen necessary to keep servicemen reasonably comfortable—could all be discovered from the "size lists." When and where these lists have survived, they have become useful research tools.

Through the two hundred years of our history the content of service records has been changed by law many times. Official service records of the men who have fought in all our wars have been compiled, each succeeding set of records more complete than the last. Not only have the records of service been changed, but the benefits accruing to veterans as well. The colonies declared their independence on 4 July 1776. On August 26 of that same year the first veterans' benefits legislation was enacted for the American colony-states as a group. The Continental Congress passed a bill providing half pay for officers and enlisted men, including men on warships and armed merchant vessels who became disabled in service and were thus incapable of earning a living. Records of these acts and the beneficiaries entitled to them have been maintained to the present time.

Basically the Federal government has provided three principal types of benefits for servicemen and their dependents: (1) disability or invalid pensions, (2) service pensions to those who served for a specified length of time, and (3) widows' pensions to widows of men who had been killed in war or who had served for a specified time. Applications made to qualify for service benefits have always had to have proof submitted for any statement made in the application.

In the days before photocopies, veterans or their widows sent original Bible records, diaries, letters, discharge papers, deeds, wills, and marriage and other records to Washington to substantiate their claims to a pension. Many a missing family Bible record has been found in pension and bounty-land warrant application files. This kind of documentation has received the special attention it deserves. Most of it has been removed for safety, some to the Library of Congress and some to special files in the National Archives. Some still remains in the original pension application, but when it is found it is usually removed for preservation.

Pension applications and bounty-land warrant applications (the latter from men who preferred a good piece of land for starting a new life after the war to remaining at home with a small cash pension) are genealogically valuable because they contain the veteran's own statement of his part in the war, supported by depositions from friends who served with him or who knew of his service. Many of the widows' statements offer brief but important family data, naming children and giving their ages, marital status, and economic background. The important events in a man's life history are very often found recorded and vouched for in his or his widow's pension application. They should never be overlooked, for they can re-create a large portion of the family history.

One Adams family insisted that their Pennsylvania ancestor had been born in Enfield, Connecticut. The name of the ancestor's father was unknown, but he was thought to have been of an age to serve in the Revolutionary War. It took a great deal of searching to locate a pension record, one of many with the name Adams examined at the National Archives, which gave the basic proofs needed to complete research on this hitherto unproved family line. An abstract is given here for the sake of brevity, for this set of pension application records contained many pages:

Elijah Adams, age 78, applied for a pension from Monroe, Licking County, Ohio, on 11 August 1833. He stated he enlisted in 1775 at Enfield, Conn., where he resided; that he marched from Enfield to Roxbury and Hingham. His second enlistment was for two months in the winter of 1776, again from Enfield, to which he returned. He enlisted a third time, again from Enfield, for six months in 1776 and was put into active duty in the Conn. Line aboard a row galley as a marine; rowed down to Lake Champlain to join Arnold; was taken prisoner by the British and released soon to return home to Enfield. He further stated he was a substitute for a short time for another man, then enlisted as a Sgt. for six months in the N.Y. Levies, his last enlistment which ended 1 December "in the last year of the war"; that he went to live in Tidingham, Mass. He says he was born in 1755 in Coventry, Conn., but there is no record of his birth because his family records were all burned 30 years ago. Since the Revolution he has lived in Enfield, Conn.;

moved about 1786 to Onlient Creek. N.Y.; moved about 1800 to Stafford, Conn,; moved about 1802 to Waynes Bush, N.Y.; moved about 1803 to Luzerne County, Pa.; moved about 1814 to Licking County, Ohio, where he has resided ever since.

Elijah Adams received his pension of $79.50 per year retroactively to 1830, and it continued until his death in 1843. Following his death, his wife, Sarah, applied for a widow's pension, and, when that was not granted, she applied for bounty land. Neither application was honored because she had not been married to Elijah Adams before 1790 —she was his second wife. Her depositions from friends and neighbors that form part of the voluminous record are very revealing:

Prior to her marriage she was Sarah Vails; Elijah Adams and she were married in Otsego County, N.Y. on 11 Feb. 1797 by Mr. Moore, Justice of the Peace; that the marriage is not of record because New York State did not require marriage registrations at that time; that she offers proof of her statements among which is one from Rachel Henies of Susquehanna County, Pa.

Rachel states she was 12 years old, living in the household of Sarah Vails and was taken along when Sarah and Elijah went to be married; that she lived with them until they left Luzerne County, Pa. to go west in 1814 and knew their history well. Other depositions revealed the names and dates of the children.

Checking on all the statements made in this lengthy record took considerable time, but proved the great value of such a record for the family searcher, for it tied in perfectly with what the family knew of their ancestry.

In checking service records and pension applications, you will notice that later records are better kept and have a great deal more genealogical value than those made earlier. By the time the country became involved in the Civil War, records also included burial records of soldiers and veterans in national cemeteries or the U.S. Soldiers' Home in Washington, D.C. No bounty lands were assigned to Civil War veterans; their benefits were pensions, with special considerations given them in homestead legislation. Unfortunately, the records for the men who fought with the Confederate states are not as good as those for Union soldiers, but they must not be overlooked if a man served with the South in the Civil War. No Federal pensions were granted to Confederate veterans, but eleven individual Southern states provided pensions for men who served under the Confederate flag. These records remain in the Southern states, usually in the archives in their state capitals.

Military records were compiled for men in the regular U.S. Army, Navy, and Marine Corps, for men who were professional servicemen or who enlisted as their chosen way of life. On the state level there are many military records to be found in state archives. They refer to state militia service or other kinds of state troop services. Some states have published these records; some are microfilmed; some have been published in part in genealogical magazines. A good genealogical library or the state library in any state where research is needed should be able to indicate where state militia records are kept.

In 1971 a fire in the Army, Navy, and Air Force Personnel centers in Saint Louis destroyed the compiled personnel folders of all enlisted men from 1912 to 1956, those of officers from 1917 to 1956, and those of Air Force personnel from 1917 to 1956. Some of these can be reconstructed, especially if the veteran ever asked for assistance. However, the Privacy Act of 1974 and the Freedom of Information Act of 1975 make it more difficult to acquire complete knowledge of the men who served. If the veteran is still alive, only he may obtain his record. Following his death, his wife, and after her death, their children may have access to the data, but the release authorization must be signed by the veteran or his next of kin. If a Veterans Administration claim was filed, there is likely to be more information available on the veteran, for a copy of his full personnel file may have been sent to the VA before the 1971 fire. Again, the request for help from the VA must be signed by the veteran's next of kin.

11

Census Records

Whether you find your way to census records early or late in your search depends on how much accurate data you can accumulate and document from family and local sources. Eventually, though, your analysis of family data will probably lead you to census records. Before plunging into this massive, seemingly overwhelming, resource, it is well to know something about it and how to approach it.

Census records are compilations of information about individuals and their households. "Enumerations" are numerical summaries of the various categories that were investigated. At the end of some of the sections in census records are enumerations that give the total numbers of males, females, occupations, houses, etc., found in a small political division. In common with all other records, these censuses and enumerations were made for some particular reason.

Ever since the time of David, son of Jesse and second king of Israel, there has been a fear of being counted. David's genealogy is recorded in the Bible. During his reign he ordered a census to be taken in Israel and Judah (the third census of its kind), despite a grave warning to refrain. The returns showed 800,000 men of fighting age in Israel and 500,000 in Judah. It took nine months and twenty days to collect the data. Soon after the completion of the census, 70,000 men died of the plague. (Nothing is reported of the women and children who died, but the number must have been high.) Because of the proximity of these two events —the census and the plague—it was believed that the plague was caused by the census (II Samuel 24:1–15). This belief—that disaster would strike after a man was counted and registered in a census—persisted throughout history. From that time forward people hid from, or refused to be interviewed by, the census taker. It has been suggested that this is still true, not necessarily because of fear of the plague, but because of that residual fear of unknown consequences.

In our own colonial times the fear of the results of enumeration were transplanted to America. Census records were needed in the colonies primarily for two different reasons —to determine where the people lived who were required to protect settlements and colonies from Indians and enemies of the colonial governments and to determine the various taxes that were needed to support governmental activities.

In 1764–65 a simple enumeration of people was prepared in Massachusetts, listing the numbers of males and females, blacks, Indians, and whites. They were divided into age categories: under sixteen years and above sixteen years of age. In 1820 a comment on the 1764–65 enumeration was made in the (Mass.) *Centinel:*

Mention is made in the papers of 1764–5 that the enumeration has been made and that some difficulties had occurred in it; many conscientious People believing that as the enumeration of God's chosen people of old was forbidden on divine authority, it was sinful for any People who had pretentions to that character to make an enumeration; and that they feared that famine and pestilence would follow it.

Despite this lingering fear, private religious objections by colonists did not prevent the official enumerations and census taking that were so necessary. But many censuses disappeared, either through neglect or because they were destroyed when their purposes had been fulfilled. A number do remain, however, and when they are found in state libraries or in genealogical collections or when they have been printed for the uses of historians and genealogists, they can be very valuable.

The first Federal census was taken in the United States in 1790 so that taxes could be levied and representatives apportioned according to the number of people living within state boundaries. The first census was called "Heads of Families at the First Census, 1790." Planned to be an enumeration by name of the head of every family, it was taken in all the states that comprised the Union at the time of the adoption of our Constitution. Complete schedules for each state were filed with the State Department in Washington, D.C., but when the British burned the Capitol during the War of 1812, those for Delaware, Georgia, Kentucky, New Jersey, Tennessee, and Virginia were destroyed. Since then attempts have been made, using other extant lists, to reconstruct the heads of families in those states just named.

Many difficulties were encountered in taking that first census. In the first place, no one had any experience in census taking. Furthermore, already tax-burdened and still conscious of the taxes that had been imposed by England, the people feared that the census might be a way to wring more from them. Their reaction was to tell as little as possible to the enumerator. Then the old superstition concerning possible divine retribution arose again. The year 1790 was so early in our nation's history that boundaries of towns and cities had not been set, nor did owners hold clear titles to their lands; deeds for many were nonexistent and Loyalist-owned land was still in dispute in some places. These considerations, too, contributed to the people's desire to withhold information.

It's true that there are probably many errors and omissions in the first census, but the reasons behind these faults bring to light the diversity of problems faced by the newly created Federal government. In fact, the 1790 Heads of Families census is something of a minor miracle in its primitive form. Many of the problems were overcome in subsequent census records, but many more problems were also added.

The 1790 census did exactly what was intended by the constitutional proviso that created it; but because it listed the names of heads of families, it inadvertently became a tool for genealogists—a means of geographically locating a family, along with an approximation of the age groupings of all persons living in the household. Since then Federal census returns have been made every ten years. The information included did not change radically between 1790 and 1840. There was a refining of age groupings as the population and public education increased (this also aided those making projections for the number of military-aged males), but that was about all.

Between 1790 and 1850 there was little conformity in how the population was recorded. In some states no printed forms were used and the record was made on any paper available, from small private account books to large legal-size sheets. By 1850 Public Health and the well-being of the citizenry were becoming an important political consideration. It was recognized that, if the form of the return was changed, the census could reflect the nation's health. Lemuel Shattuck of Boston was made responsible for the proposed improvements in the census information, with the result that instead of a single line to describe a family unit, naming only the head of the family, each member of the family was described in a full line of information. The head of the family, his wife, children, parents if any were living in the household, servants, and slaves were now not only named, but a record was made of their ages at the last birthday before the census date. Sex, color, occupation, value of any real estate owned, place of birth, whether married, whether school was attended within the previous year; ability to read and write if over twenty-one; whether deaf, dumb, blind, insane, idiotic, a pauper, or a convict —all of these were included to determine whether the nation was composed of healthy, stable people.

The surviving census records are now properly housed in the National Archives in Washington, D.C., where microfilm copies are available to researchers. Many libraries have acquired copies of those that pertain to their own state and have often added those for contiguous states. The National Archives has published descriptive booklets on the collection, and these should be added to your personal library as a basic reference.

In the ten years between Federal censuses, many states conducted their own enumerations and census-taking halfway through the decade. They followed the Federal form quite closely, yet added some information that expanded its value to the state and consequently to the researcher. The state census records are not preserved in the National Archives but are usually found within the state of their origin, in the state archives, the state library, or in the offices of County Clerks, with copies in the state library or in historical and genealogical libraries. Copies of any census collected in the territories are in the National Archives in Washington, D.C.

The value of census records to the genealogist varies according to the date of the record, since they are not consistent in content. Information was supposed to be furnished by an individual. Congress stipulated that it should be furnished by the head of the family, recognizing the head of the family as the husband or father unless he was deceased. Because husbands and fathers are usually poor sources of ages and birth dates within a household, this led to numerous inaccuracies.

If there was an older person in good health in the household, his or her age was frequently estimated to be too young by a son- or daughter-in-law. An older person in poor health was frequently estimated to be older than he actually was. Some families believed to have lived in a particular place at a particular time may not be found on a census because they were away from home on the day the census taker visited them and he did not return to get the necessary information. Others, who believed that to be enumerated meant that there would be a death in the family within a year, hid when the government man was in the vicinity.

In the 1880 census, the place of origin is recorded. If, as so often happened, the head of the family was at work when the enumerator arrived, his place of origin might be incorrectly stated by the informant because it wasn't definitely known. Sometimes the recorder used ditto marks down the column rather than taking the time to write in the name of the state or country of origin. We cannot say now that the recorder was dishonest, but as we become experienced in using census records, we can be sure that some were very careless. Certain of the discrepancies we find are not the fault of the recorder, however.

Acknowledgment of age is still a problem for some people, but giving inaccurate data to a recorder borders on the ridiculous.

Women, in particular, have been guilty in this respect on the census records. They tended to minimize their ages, not wanting to appear to be as old as, or older than, their husbands. Checking ages against other records reveals some startling differences that make the researcher wonder whether it was because the woman gave an inaccurate age, or whether she spoke too softly for the recorder to hear properly. The census taker was usually someone who knew the area in which he worked, or was native to it, which may account for some of the poor information he obtained from its inhabitants.

It must not be concluded from these warnings that census records have little value for the genealogist. Quite the contrary. Through them we can trace complete households, beginning in 1850 when all members of the family were first listed and moving forward or backward into other census records. By following the family in later records, we can learn how they broke into other units, settling nearby or moving on. Within the family an older person of a different name may give the clue to the maiden name of the mother of the household. The economic status of the family, the degree of education, the occupation, the place of origin—all these and much more can be learned in later census records. Often a clue obtained in this way will lead to information about other unknown members of the family who lived nearby. It is well to add this to your notes so that you won't have to research the same census again.

When the census was being taken, the recorder usually worked along a street or road so that the names of relatives who lived nearby could be learned. This, too, could be helpful, for when a family moved from one area to another, it was often with relatives or neighbors who made the same move. In going from New York State to Ohio, for instance, several families from one area would purchase land close to each other in Ohio and make the overland trip together. Finding the same names on census records first in one place and then on the next census in another area is an encouraging clue. For this reason it is always a good idea to take from a census not only the family name sought but his neighbors' names as well. As pointed out earlier, propinquity played a large part in marriages. It would follow that the names of the neighbors who lived contiguous to your family, or moved on with your people, might provide the heretofore unknown maiden name of a wife.

Not all census takers have been excellent penmen, and reading their handwriting is not always easy. If you will take time to examine a page that has been written by one person, discovering some of the idiosyncrasies of his writing style will help you to read single entries more readily. Perhaps he used forms of T and F that could be confused, or his terminal r and n were similar in appearance. Perhaps his o looked like an a, or his n like a u. Some of the earlier census takers still practiced old forms in which a double s gave the appearance of being a combination of f and s. If you will look at a page of notes you have recently written, you will discover that your note-taking handwriting leaves much to be desired, too. How, then, can we remain annoyed with census takers whose handwriting is not always legible?

Census taking was not a well-paid job, and it could be tedious and demanding, for more than one handwritten copy had to be made. This caused Tho's A. Jerome to write on the last page of the census return for the Third Ward of New York City in 1850, "God knows I am Glad I am finished End of one extra copy. And I Hope when congress passes another law they will pay better for the doing it." Poorly paid, not always fully literate, men have done a colossal job of preserving for us our heritage. We owe them a great deal.

PART THREE
Loose Ends

12

Pitfalls

This chapter could have been labeled "Beginner, beware!" but many of the difficulties beginners meet in genealogy are never conquered even by more skilled searchers. Perhaps if you are aware of them from the beginning you will achieve more with less error and frustration. Some of the pitfalls have already been mentioned, but they bear repeating.

Among your first activities was that of gathering information from your family. These probably included several "family traditions." Four of these that seem most persistent present a triple threat to the unwary.

The first is the "three brothers who came to America" tradition. Too many genealogies begin with this statement, then continue by tracing one or two and ignoring the third brother. The searcher is convinced that he descends from that third, undiscovered brother and proceeds to try to trace a

159

line from him to himself—in the wrong direction. It is better to arrive at the third brother by the more acceptable reverse method—if he ever existed. Research may prove that it was not just three brothers who came to the colony, but a whole family group in which the older members were too busy clearing land and getting settled to have left any records. The Todd family of Somerset County, New Jersey, supposedly stems from three brothers who migrated from Longford in northern Ireland in 1749. However, in 1727 these three brothers, with two more brothers and a sister, were listed as "old customers" in the ledgers of the local general store.

The second tradition concerns the three-brother syndrome also, only this time they are said to have been "shipwrecked twelve miles off the coast." It seems always to be "twelve miles"! One brother was picked up by a fortuitously passing fisherman; one supposedly swam to shore; one was presumed "lost in the shipwreck, but may be the founder of our family" in some other colony or state. Of course you will question that twelve-mile swim, as well as all the other possibilities inherent in the story, the most unlikely being the "passing fisherman."

The third is the "we are descended from royalty" tradition. This is a very persistent statement and in many cases a provable one. Some genealogists claim that if family lines are traced far enough, everyone is descended from nobility or royalty of some country, because in earlier times there were fewer people in the world. However, the searcher must not take the statement of descent from royalty literally. Like all traditions, it may have a grain of truth in it, but implicit faith in such a statement demands proof, with a solidly documented line back to the claimed royalty. Anneke Jans, one of the early Dutch ladies of New Amsterdam and wife of the famous Domine Everardus Bogardus, has been reported over and over again to have been the granddaughter of William the Silent of the Netherlands; but the record shows that she was from an island off the coast of Scandinavia and not even remotely of royal blood. Bragging about an unsubstantiated tradition is in even worse taste than bragging about a documented claim.

The fourth tradition is the "unreclaimed-family-fortune" one. The belief is that a fortune has been left behind in the old country and that it will soon fall to the family in America because they are the only known descendants. Futile hopes and dreams have been built on this tradition. Actually, although there may have been a bit of truth to this at first, when fortunes or lands are "unreclaimed" they are returned to the crown or government within a few years. There has been a great deal of money unwisely spent by families when approached by unscrupulous lawyers and others who claim that they can obtain the family fortune for the living descendants. To spend money on such a will-o'-the-wisp is foolish and shortsighted, since there are too many variables involved.

Another problem for beginners and more advanced searchers is that they can become confused by finding two people with the same name living in the same area. About the only way to differentiate between people with duplicate names is through careful checking of the records available, using arithmetical computations carefully and seeking firm documentation. You may then find that they are cousins, or that one is a more distant relative of another family. One may be young, another older, but it can be difficult to figure out who is who. Frequently they are even married to wives with similar first names.

Surnames have various ethnic backgrounds

and may have suffered in translation or transcription. Some of us are familiar with the changes wrought in family names at the time of immigration. Grabowski became Grabb; Zuzzulo became Zuzuro; Tarrace became Tarr; Lebenstein became Livingston; Goldstein became Goldstone; Petrova became Stone; Casablanca became Whitehouse. The immigrant may have translated his name himself as he adopted the ways of his new country. Zimmermann translated to Carpenter; Schneider to Cutter or Taylor; Casseboom to Cherrytree. Name changes of this kind can lead to time-wasting search unless someone in the family has retained, or reverted to, the original form of the name.

Given names have as many variable spellings or mutations as do surnames. Margaret may become Marj, Meg, or Peg. Mary has taken many forms: Molly, Polly, Marie, Maria, Maryte. Nicholas turns into Nick, Claus, and other forms, while Jacobus is sometimes shortened to Jake or Jacob, or translated as James. Johannes and John may appear in the same family as brothers; but whereas John usually continues in that form, Johannes may evolve into Hannes, Hans, Johan, and other forms.

One family whose name was Gott thought

that they were of German origin, since "Gott" is the German word for "God." However, it was eventually learned that the name was of English origin and had been Gutt, referring to the occupation of an ancestor who was a butcher. The study of names is a whole field of interest in itself, and many books and articles have been written on the subject.

Mistakes are sometimes made in recognizing that a "von" or "van" or "de" has either been dropped from a name or ostentatiously added to it. Actually, all three prefixes signified a place of origin, as de France, von Heine, or van Amsterdam.

Saying a name out loud will often give a clue to the country of origin, especially if one has a slight knowledge of the language involved. The German Bickle turned into Pickle in America; the Dutch Vreelandt became Freeland. Even the English name Freman evolved into Freeman. Don't let the many ways a name is spelled disconcert you. Spelling depended on the pronunciation of a name as it was heard by the person who wrote it. This in turn depended on the scribe's prior knowledge of how he had seen it written, or whether he was familiar with the language from which it came. So simple a name as Mott, with just four letters, has been found with over a dozen spellings, and other more complicated names have been found with over twenty-five different spellings. All such changes should be noted and the name sought in indexes under all the known spellings.

Styles in names change from generation to generation, but in an area where children are named for a popular local hero, a minister, or a doctor, differentiating among them can be difficult. It is also sometimes found that similarly named children were named for a well-loved member of the family whom everyone admired. It may be that several first cousins are found with similar given names, occasioned by the fact that they all had a well-to-do grandparent and the parents hoped that by naming the child for him, that child would be remembered in his will. A search for a great-grandfather brought out the fact that there were seven men named Peter Bogart living within a ten-mile area at the same time: four Peter Bogart, Sr.'s, one son named Peter, Jr., and two grandsons named Peter II. One of these families was most easily documented, but was not the family needed. The remaining six had to be investigated carefully. After involved research following every possible clue, a family was found still living in that area that claimed descent from a Peter Bogart through one of his daughters. A visit was arranged and data were compared proving that the "right" Peter had been found. It had taken nearly ten years, but the correct line was established and two families were led to reestablish familial relationships that had ended more than a century before.

Another pitfall is the change that has occurred in the meanings of words signifying relationships. Found in wills or deeds, especially, is the word "nephew," which sometimes meant grandson, (since it originally came from the Latin word "nepos", meaning "grandson"). "Cousin" very often meant any blood relative. The term "in-law" included adopted or step relatives, while sister or brother meant not only blood relatives of the same parents (siblings), but were also ecclesiastical terms that included brothers or sisters in a religious denomination.

The pitfall of generation designation can cause great confusion. "Junior" was a term applied to the younger of two persons of the same name in the same location, but not necessarily closely related. In New England, records have been found with such designations as "John Smith III, formerly John

Smith IV," indicating that there were formerly four of the same name in the area. If one died or moved away, one of the remaining three might even be called "Junior."

Time moved with the same regularity for our ancestors as it does for us, and human error in gauging time hasn't changed. Therefore, for the family historian, dates and time spans must be carefully scrutinized before acceptance. This is the place where the use of "possibly" and "probably" and "about" are most frequently used in preparing notes.

When a date is written "b. c. 1790," "d. about 1870," "m. c. 1840" (born circa 1790, died about 1870, married circa 1840), it is too easy to drop the "circa" or the "about," to accept the year and write it in all future records as "b. 1790"; "d. 1870"; "m. 1840." Not only is this careless transcription, it is dishonest, for a correction is being made without proof. Be sure to copy dates or anything else exactly as you find them, keep an accurate note concerning where you located the information, and later, when you have more data and can prove your point, write the dates or any other facts as you believe them to be, stating your proofs.

The Julian calendar that placed New Year's

Day on March 25 was in use in Britain and her colonies until 1752, though other countries had long since accepted the newer calendar. In 1752 the British adopted the Gregorian calendar, which placed New Year's Day on the first of January. This change from Julian (Old Style) to Gregorian (New Style) had considerable impact and created special problems for the genealogist and family historian. Double-dating became necessary: 22 March 1720/21. This shows that by Old Style (O.S.) the date was actually 22 March 1720, but counting it as New Style (N.S.) the date was 22 March 1721. This same date may be written 22 March 1720 O.S. or 22 March 1721 N.S., as may any other date prior to 1752. All dates for the first half of the eighteenth century should be double-dated to ensure accuracy, or singly marked O.S. or N.S. prior to 25 March 1752.

People who use numerals for recording months, days, and years create hazards for the unwary. Does the 75 in 8/7/75 mean 1775, 1875, or 1975? If we are not certain of the period in which dates are being sought, even the month and day can seem interchangeable in number transcription. Does the 8/7 mean August 7 or July 8? Only by writing dates in the acceptable genealogical manner can this kind of pitfall be avoided: 7 July 1875—the day in numeral, followed by month written out, and year clearly defined.

Marriage dates were recorded in three ways: by date of the license issued, by date of publication of intention to marry (the date of banns published in courthouse or church), and by the date of the marriage itself. Published volumes such as *New York Marriages Previous to 1784* list the date of the license or bond. The marriage could have taken place at any time within the next two weeks; therefore, the license, banns, or intention dates should not be given as the marriage date. Clear identification of birth, marriage, divorce, and death dates are all civil matters regulated by law, and therefore public records have been created to list them. Ecclesiastical records have been created to cover the church's participation in these vital matters. Therefore, records of baptism, marriage, and burial are found in church records. When the family historian records vital events, the date should be clearly defined as to whether it is birth (b.) or baptism (bap.), death (d.) or burial (bur.), license (lic.) or banns (bns.) or marriage (m.).

Arithmetical probabilities are pitfalls that

can be amusing or sadly misleading. A man born about 1810, married about 1835 to a woman his own age, is probably not going to be the father of children born before 1823 or after 1870. Simple arithmetical subtraction and common sense would show that this couple would probably have children between 1836 and 1855, although the wife's childbearing years might be stretched to 1860. Margins of your notes are a good place to avoid this pitfall; use them to do frequent addition and subtraction problems.

It is wise to learn what was happening nationally and locally at the time a private family event took place. A man who fought in the Pequot War cannot be expected to appear as a hero in records of the Revolution. A man who fought in the Civil War cannot be expected to appear in the 1912 Mexican border incident. Generations are roughly computed at thirty years, although there are many families who prove to be exceptions by marrying early and crowding two or more generations into thirty or thirty-five years.

Incorrect information concerning ages of females has been a joke among comedians for many years. Anyone doing genealogical research will discover that females have not been the only ones to be perpetrators or victims of this kind of hoax. Males have exaggerated their ages to obtain a license, or so that they will not appear on a record as younger than their wives. Death records for both males and females give incorrect ages, sometimes because the one giving the information doesn't really know, or because the deceased allowed a false age to be popularly known and accepted for him. Search becomes imperative for more than one piece of evidence to establish a correct vital date.

If you want to be a good family historian, you must be a Doubting Thomas (or Thomasina). Until you have learned from experience where the pitfalls lie, be thorough —search diligently for more than one record to confirm a date or a fact.

At the Water's Edge

One thing virtually all citizens of the United States share is the fact that we are descendants of immigrants. Some of our ancestors left their native country several generations before others, but no matter how long ago or how recently our people set out for the New World, they were all immigrants. Eventually, we, their descendants, must come to the water's edge and seek records from across the seas. There are some who wish only to prove their lines in America, but others will want to push into their origins as far back as possible. How can this be done? It isn't as hopeless a task as so many have been led to believe.

The first step in building your family history was to consult every member of your family, recording all the information you could extract from them about names, places, dates, and relationships. If you did this as thoroughly as you should, you may have uncovered the information you will need as a basis for search abroad, for most immigrants carefully kept their identification papers after arriving in America. At least one of their children should have been interested enough to have kept those papers, either for sentimental reasons or as a tangible link with their unknown past. Search diligently among all the relatives for papers such as exit certificates or newspaper clippings from the old country that advertised the intention to leave. Look for passports, naturalization papers, and old letters from relatives and friends left behind. Among the foreign language or religious newspapers in this country you may be able to find an obituary that gives information about the origin of the deceased. Any or all of these can produce clues to correlate with stories and traditions you heard when you talked with family members.

It may not be necessary for you to enter a campaign of writing or visiting abroad. There has been so much interest in our origins that the very data you need may already have been made available here. The Genealogical Society of the Church of Jesus Christ of Latter-day Saints at Salt Lake City, Utah (Mormons), has a continuing program of collecting microfilm copies of vital records from all over the world. To use this collection, you may want to go to Salt Lake City to do research. No fees are charged for the use of the material at the Genealogical Society there. Or, if you live near a "stake library" of this organization, you may visit it and receive the same help. Stake libraries have catalogs of the microfilms at Salt Lake City. You may select from them the microfilms you want to consult, whether of foreign or domestic records, pay a nominal fee, and the microfilm will be sent to the local stake library. You will be notified of its arrival and may then go to the library to use it. In Salt Lake City there are persons at the Genealogical Society who can read the foreign languages and translate for you. The Society also maintains a roster of genealogists qualified to do research in foreign records on microfilms at Salt Lake City for a reasonable fee. The Society continues to publish its Research Paper Series that began in 1966. Copies can be found in large libraries and in branch libraries of the Society. They give information on what types of records exist in foreign countries, what kind of genealogical information they contain, and whether they are available for research.

Various National Information Services

maintaining offices in New York City have published booklets telling how to search for your ancestors in their countries. Canada, the Scandinavian countries, Germany, and others offer this service.

Instead of going abroad yourself, it is possible, for a very reasonable fee, to obtain the services of researchers who will do the work for you over there. Their names can be obtained from their advertisements in the more important American genealogical magazines, which you can consult in a library. When you write to a researcher, be sure to enclose two International Coupons for postage instead of United States stamps. These coupons are for sale at U.S. Post Offices for a few cents. They permit your researcher to obtain the proper stamps of his own country for his reply to you via airmail at no cost to him.

Many books have been written to help our understanding of overseas research. Some are for specific countries; others will help develop a general background of knowledge of the problems involved. Available in most genealogical libraries and large libraries, these books may be helpful.

In addition to books, you may find it of great help to consult the genealogical magazines before you go overseas to search. One young woman who decided to trace her new husband's family established his line back to the first person of the name in this country, who had settled in Pennsylvania. She decided that the European origin of the family would have to wait until she and her husband could afford a vacation trip abroad. A month or two later a genealogical magazine published an article in which the author documented the background of the family for at least three generations in Europe before its migration here.

There are a few warnings that should be noted before you decide to do research abroad either through the services of a researcher or do-it-yourself:

1. Be sure that you have the correct spelling of the family name as it would have been spelled originally before any Americanizing changes were made in it. This applies also to the given names of immigrants—Jean Maes from France became John Mace when he emigrated to America, but his vital records in France remained in his original name.

2. Geographical locations have not changed, but national boundary lines have. A place of origin may no longer belong to

the same country it did when the immigrants left for America. Check this carefully.

3. English is a universal language now, but it is still a courtesy to address letters of inquiry in the language of the recipient. If you have not retained the family's original language as one of your own, write a succinct letter asking for information in English, and have it translated before mailing.

4. If you have been unable to find any clues concerning the exact place of origin of your family, study the migration patterns of the particular time you know your family came to the United States.

5. Check the friends and neighbors of your family in this country, because they were often friends and neighbors in the old country who emigrated at the same time. It is always possible that they or their children have kept records that may provide a valuable clue.

6. Be sure to exhaust all publications, books, periodicals, and pamphlets published in the United States before either writing or going abroad. One very skilled European researcher told me that he frequently received three-page letters from Americans asking for help. He would be able to go to his card file and reply with a one-line letter telling

the correspondent that the information he needed was published on a certain page of an American genealogical magazine!

A trip abroad to do your own searching can be rewarding, especially if there is no language barrier, but you will need to be prepared with knowledge of the location and existence of the records you want to consult well beforehand.

Too many Americans of Jewish parentage believe that their lineage cannot be traced. This may be true in some instances, but that is no excuse for not putting together a family history of what can be collected. The Jews were among the earliest genealogists in the world. Like the Maoris in the Pacific Islands and the Incas in Peru, they learned their pedigrees in each generation and could repeat them by rote. It is a tradition that has been neglected in modern times, but the American Jewish Archives in Cincinnati, Ohio, is deeply interested in the genealogy of the Jews in America. Dr. Malcolm H. Stern, Genealogist of the American Jewish Archives, has published from their records a massive book of family charts showing lines of descent from immigrants who came to this country. The American Jewish Archives is constantly seeking family information from Jewish descendants. Their records are open to serious researchers.

As the recent blockbuster *Roots* witnessed, the black American is finding that it is not impossible for him to build a family history. It is accomplished in exactly the same way all family pedigrees are compiled, by starting with oneself and collecting information from family and relatives, using all the records available in this country. It may be that the family will be traceable only to plantation records, but if there are clues remaining in the family, it is possible to prove lines back to Africa. Alex Haley, author of *Roots*, achieved results through hard work and persistence. Libraries are becoming increasingly conscious of the growth of interest in black history, which goes hand in hand with growing interest in black genealogy. Not a great deal has been published, but as the search goes on, more and more help will become available. Meanwhile, just to collect all possible genealogical data on your own family as far as you can go will be of importance to those descendants who want the answers to the who, where, and when, that you can supply—and that will be lost if you don't write it down now.

These arguments are valid for recent immigrants to America. Busy with adjustments to life in the United States, their rich cultural heritage and family pedigrees may not seem important now, but if what is known and remembered by the first and second generations of emigrants into this country is preserved in writing, their descendants will have a base on which to build their story for future generations.

Books to Help the Beginner

Each book listed here contains a bibliography that should be consulted for help on specific problems. You may examine them at libraries or purchase copies for yourself. It is also wise to familiarize yourself with publications of genealogical and historical societies in the specific geographic areas where your people settled.

Baxter, Angus. *In Search of Your Roots: A Guide for Canadians Seeking Their Ancestors*. Revised and updated. Toronto: Macmillan of Canada, 1984.

——. *In Search of Your British & Irish Roots: A Complete Guide to Tracing Your English, Welsh, Scottish, and Irish Ancestors*. Toronto: Macmillan of Canada, 1982; Baltimore: Genealogical Publishing Co., Inc., 1986 (paperback edition).

——. *In Search of Your European Roots: A Complete Guide to Tracing Your Ancestors in Every Country in Europe*. Baltimore: Genealogical Publishing Co., Inc., 1985.

————. *In Search of Your German Roots: A Complete Guide to Tracing Your Ancestors in the Germanic Areas of Europe.* Baltimore: Genealogical Publishing Co., Inc., 1987.
The four books by Angus Baxter provide detailed instructions for locating records abroad, with emphasis on conducting research by mail. Very useful in cutting through the complexities of foreign research.

Doane, Gilbert H. *Searching for Your Ancestors: The How and Why of Genealogy.* 5th ed. (with James B. Bell). Minneapolis: University of Minnesota Press, and Boston: New England Historic Genealogical Society, 1980.
A very readable, excellent introduction to genealogical research. It is based on long experience in New England records, but it also contains a chapter on preparing to do research abroad.

Eakle, Arlene and Johni Cerny. *The Source: A Guidebook of American Genealogy.* Salt Lake City: Ancestry Publishing Company, 1984.
A major anthology compiled by the editors and fourteen specialists who have crammed

their collective expertise into a massive, small print, valuable compendium. Well indexed.

Everton, George B., Sr., *The Handy Book for Genealogists*. 7th ed. Logan, Utah: The Everton Publishers, Inc., 1981.
Contains state and county histories, maps, a list of libraries, where to write for records, etc. Periodically revised and updated.

Greenwood, Val D. *The Researcher's Guide to American Genealogy*. Baltimore: Genealogical Publishing Co., Inc., 1973.
An encyclopedic volume and an all-purpose reference, generally regarded as the standard text in American genealogy.

Hilton, Suzanne. *Who Do You Think You Are? Digging for Your Family Roots*. Philadelphia: Westminster Press, 1976.
Written for and addressed to the high school student.

Jacobus, Donald Lines. *Genealogy as Pastime and Profession*. 2nd ed. Baltimore: Genealogical Publishing Co., Inc., 1968.
This anthology of articles by one of the most skilled genealogists of the twentieth century is for beginners and experienced alike.

Kurzweil, Arthur. *From Generation to Generation: How to Trace Your Jewish Genealogy and Personal History*. New York: William Morrow and Company, Inc., 1980.
Emphasizing East European Jewish genealogy, this excellent how-to book comes in a paperback edition from Schocken Books.

Rose, James M. and Alice Eichholz. *Black Genesis*. Detroit: Gale Research, 1976.
A comprehensive guide to black records and methods of black research.

Rubincam, Milton, ed. *Genealogical Research: Methods and Sources*. Rev. ed. Vol. I. Washington, D.C.: The American Society of Genealogists, 1980.
A collection of articles by outstanding members of this society on various phases of genealogy. It contains chapters on research in each of the original states. Volume II, edited by Kenn Stryker-Rodda (rev. ed., 1983), contains chapters on research in the states west to the Mississippi Valley and on research in Ontario, on Huguenot and Jewish migrations, and on black genealogy.

Stryker-Rodda, Kenn. *Genealogy*. Boy Scouts

of America. A Merit Badge pamphlet.
A simple, clear instruction booklet that embodies all important methods of research for Americans of any age.

Wright, Norman E. *Preserving Your American Heritage: A Guide to Family and Local History*. Provo, Utah: Brigham Young University Press, 1981.
A revision of *Building an American Pedigree* (1974), this guide contains photocopies of virtually every type of record a genealogist is likely to consult, plus a fine series of maps and extensive bibliographies. Since the author conducts courses in genealogy at Brigham Young University, his book is written from the Latter-day Saints' viewpoint, but his sound methodology makes the volume valuable to all researchers.

A note on the text
Large print edition designed by
Kipling West.
Composed in 18 pt Plantin
on a Xyvision 300/Linotron 202N
by Tara McSherry Casey
of G.K. Hall & Co.